I Got A "D" In
Leadership

I Got A "D" In Leadership

Anyone Can Lead

Allen Chapin

ISBN- 13: 9781548652753
ISBN: 154865275X
Library of Congress Control Number: 2017910781
CreateSpace Independent Publishing Platform
North Charleston, South Carolina

Printed in the United States of America

*This book is dedicated to
those leaders who have been
willing to come alongside me
with their leadership "D's"
so that my dreams
could become reality*

CONTENTS

SECTION 1

IDENTIFYING THE PLAYERS

INTRODUCTION

ANYONE CAN LEAD. There. I said it. Well, I wrote it. And to tell the truth, those may have been the three most difficult words to write in this book. Difficult, not because I didn't know where to start, but because most people don't believe those words are true. Many people believe that leaders are born. They believe that only certain people are cut out for leadership roles.

But I am an eternal optimist. I believe anything is possible... at least with God. I believe anyone can lead. Regardless of background, personality, upbringing, economic status, gender, or race, anyone can lead. You can lead.

If you don't believe it, then the book in your hand has the potential to transform your life. It has the potential to open new doors of opportunity to you. It has the potential to catapult you into leadership in a way that you may not have believed was possible before. And it has the potential to help you elevate someone else into leading like they never believed possible.

If you truly do believe those three little words... Anyone can lead... then you already have the heart of this book within you.

So, why keep reading? Because for you, this book has the potential to put tools in your hands to build other leaders... to build great teams to accomplish more than anyone could alone.

GRADES OR GIFTS?

I was a good student. No, really, I was. Well, I was a good student in grade school... and in middle school. Hey, I was even a good student in high school. Advanced classes, honor roll, National Honor Society, 4.0+ GPA. (Well, except for Geometry, but let's skip that little detail.)

Yet things shifted a little as I moved into my college years. I actually had to study to be a good student. And while I maintained A's & B's, my two-year stint at the local junior college with two different majors was unimpressive.

I took a year off traditional schooling, as I began to once again answer the call of God on my life to vocational ministry, and launched into eight distance education courses to begin the process of procuring my ministerial credentials. Result? Epic fail. I was not disciplined enough at that point in my life to know how to balance work and self-study classes... and fun.

But as the Lord would have it, that soul-searching year of accomplishing half of one course actually propelled me toward the Christian university where I would gain my undergrad degree. That degree didn't come easily, though. I had this faulty philosophy that said, "Why should I work so hard to get A's when I can have fun and get B's?"

Again, epic fail. Oh, sure I got A's in some classes when I really enjoyed the professor or the course material. But I did not apply myself in some other really important classes within my major and ended up barely passing them with D's.

I'm not proud of those D's. In fact, they glare at me from my transcript. They mock me. They sneer at me from my past. Don't get me wrong... I learned in those courses, but more from accident than from purposeful effort. Fortunately for me, God is gracious, and most people don't ask to see my transcript. Plus, there is now Google and a whole slough of Bible study software available to help me out.

But there is one "D" that I received along the way of which I am truly proud. I got a "D" in leadership. No, it was not a leadership course I took in college. Rather, it is a life course in which I am enrolled permanently. And if you're reading this book, then you are most likely enrolled in it as well because this is a book for leaders. The odd thing with this major is that, once you enroll, you never really graduate. Instead, you move from course to course, building on what you learned in previous courses.

That is exactly what has happened with me. I have been leading, or influencing, since I was a pre-teen. But it wasn't until I made it to my early forties that I discovered I got a "D" in leadership. After years of studying and learning about leadership, I had an epiphany of sorts— a revelation if you will— when it came to understanding that each of us can lead, regardless of which "D" we received in leadership.

You see, you may not realize it, but you've also received a "D" in leadership. Please don't misunderstand what I am saying. I don't mean in any way to insult you or your leadership abilities. You're probably a terrific leader... A phenomenal leader... An amazing leader. It's just the premise that drives this book... the fact that we each get a "D" in leadership.

What you need to understand though, is that this "D" isn't a grade. This is not something you have earned. This is not the measure of your ability or aptitude. It's a gift you're given. Like God's grace, God's gifts are just that... gifts. We don't earn them. He simply gives them.

You may have had some teachers in school, like I did over the years, who started the semester or year off by telling the class that he or she does not give grades, but rather we as students earn the grades we get. And while that is true of formal education with instruction and testing, what we're about to pursue with our time together in this book is not about you (or me for that matter) learning information that we will be tested on later. We will indeed be instructed, and my guess is that God will be kind enough to give us the opportunity to test whether or not we have absorbed this information into our hearts and minds. But it would be more accurate to say that this book is about a revelation of truth which will set you free to become the leader you desire to be, and maybe more importantly, to help those leaders whom you lead become the best leaders they can possibly become.

You see, our leadership "D" is a designation. It is an identifier. It is a classification to help us better define who we are as leaders and help us better align ourselves within a team for success as leaders. It is God's gift to help us be the most effective at influencing those around us in this world whom we have been given the privilege to impact for eternity. As a gift, we simply need to accept it and learn how to best utilize it.

I don't know about you, but I love tech gadgets. I know, that probably makes me a little geeky, but I never said that I was the coolest, most suave guy in the world. And yet I have a problem with the very tech toys I enjoy. What's my problem with tech toys? I hate to read the instructions. It can come with a instructional video & I still probably won't want to take time to watch it. I just want to be able to pick it up and use it immediately. Now, I know that it is sometimes just laziness. I get it. And I normally press on through... by asking someone else to show me how to use it. Because how crazy would I have to be if my amazing wife gave me a tech toy for my birthday, but I didn't learn how to use it? It would be a useless gift, a paperweight in a digital world.

And yet, the same is true of these "D's" which God gives us. We can accept them, but we need to learn how to best utilize them. So, through the course of this book, it is my hope that you will both learn what your leadership "D" is, and then also learn how to lead from that role, regardless of your title or assignment.

DIFFERENT "D'S"

Let me break it down for you right here at the beginning. There are five different "D's", one of which each of us most easily fit into as it relates to our leadership. (I'll spell them out in the next chapter as we get ready to look at each of them individually.) Unfortunately, we sometimes think our title or role defines which "D" we have instead of discovering our "D" and leading from that place on the team.

The truth is, most of us desire to lead well. We want to be the best leaders we possibly can, but we often confuse leading with having a particular role, or skill set, or title. John Maxwell has written, "Leadership is not about titles, positions or flowcharts. It is about one life influencing another."[1]

If that is true, then I would like to suggest that we can each be a primary leader in whatever position or role we have, regardless of which "D" we received in leadership. Your skill set may not clearly fit your title, or vice versa. More may be required of you than you feel like you can bring to the table. Don't let that concern you.

Think about it this way... Most of us consider that a leader must be a visionary, type-A, commander, lion, driven personality. And on top of that, the truth is that we probably expect even more of those serving as the primary leader. We might expect that person to have tons of amazing ideas, to be great at thinking out processes, to be great at delegating assignments, and/or even to be a get-the-job-done person.

But not every leader brings all those things into their role. In fact, very few of us are multi-talented geniuses that can do almost anything. (I mean, not everyone can be like us. wink, wink). Instead, if we're not careful, most of us end up as leaders who are jacks-of-all-trades-masters-of-none, tackling whatever is put in front of us and just trying to make it all happen... usually, with little success in any of it.

To our own dismay, most of us are not equipped to accomplish everything that needs to be accomplished by a well-rounded leadership team. So we end up feeling like ineffective leaders... failures. What we need to discover instead is which "D" we've been given and then surround ourselves with the other four leadership "D's" which we need on our team in order to be successful.

This concept of various roles of leadership ability is nothing new. Go back to the book of Exodus in Scripture and there you can find Moses trying to lead millions of Israelites from bondage in Egypt to a new life in the Promised Land. In those accounts from Scripture, we find a guy who was raised in a king's palace and talked with God like a man talks with his friend. This guy worked miracles. His face glowed from his personal times of being alone in the presence of God for extended periods. If anyone could handle multiple roles of leadership, it ought to have been Moses.

But when his father-in-law, Jethro, comes to visit the grandkids, he finds Moses frazzled & overwhelmed. Jethro sits back for a little while... takes it all in, watching all that Moses is doing as a leader... assesses the situation... and then finally decides that something has to be said if something is going to get done.

Praise God for godly, wise fathers-in-law. My father-in-law has given me some incredible advice over the years that has probably saved me from losing my mind, my ministry, or my marriage. Many an hour has been spent in that 16-foot Gator fishing boat with him coaching me and mentoring me through leadership challenges while we wet a hook in hopes of landing the big one. Along the way, he has cautioned me, challenged me, encouraged me and even gently called me out.

That's the kind of father-in-law Moses had. Jethro was a man who could look the man of God in the face and tell him that there is a more effective way to lead.

Moses wasn't the only one who learned this lesson. The disciples heard Jesus teach on the parable of talents and took notes. Everyone gets something, but not everyone gets the same thing. The book of Acts shows that they learned the lesson. When the ball gets dropped in reaching out to needy widows, they discover that they as apostles have one "D" and need some other leaders with the other "D's" added to their team so that they could be the most effective at impacting this world for the Kingdom of our Lord.

So, what do you do when you are asked... or challenged... or maybe even expected to lead, and yet you don't consider yourself to be a dream-having, vision-casting, miracle-working, fast-running leader? What do you do when you don't personally have a multi-talented skill set, but you are still called upon to lead? What do you do when the team of leaders you lead doesn't seem to have all the pieces of the puzzle to really operate at the highest levels of excellence?

I'd like to suggest that you learn to be the leader you were created to be and lead from that place of strength. God knows who you are and how He created you. He understands the personality type He gave you. He knows how you are wired. He is well aware of your strengths and weaknesses. He knows what make you tick, what electrifies you, what motivates you.

In fact, He gave you a "D" in leadership. And that's a good thing. It's actually a great thing! If you understood how great it is that He gave you a "D", you would be on the edge of your seat right now as you are reading this book, and you would be begging for me to get on with it.

So I will... Get on with it, that is. Over the next one hundred thirty pages or so, you'll discover that each leader falls into one of five leadership categories. On top of that, I believe you'll find that you can be a great leader— a person of significant influence— who can lead an entire team of leaders regardless of which "D" you have received in leadership. In fact, I believe that, if you can identify which type of leader you are, then you can make an even more profound impact in the lives of those you influence, all the while enjoying your leadership role more and more.

So, why not pause with me right now and let's invite the Lord to get involved in this process with us? Maybe you're not a Christian. This book is still for you, and everything in it won't be real preachy or churchy

Maybe you've never thought about talking with God or asking Him to get involved with your leadership. That's okay. Believe it or not, He's always listening and He would love to hear your voice. Here's a prayer you could use to help get the conversation started:

Lord, thank You for choosing me to lead. I accept that my leadership role is no accident. I believe that I am the right person for this role at this time. I also admit that I need You to point out the most effective way for me to lead. I trust You to reveal to me which "D" You have chosen to give me as a leader. Please speak clearly to me as I read through this book, helping me to understand how to be the best leader I can be in Your strength. And please help me learn how to help others lead as well. Amen.

CHAPTER 1

EVERYONE GETS A "D"

STUNNED

MY ADMINISTRATIVE ASSISTANT resigned and I panicked. I had been serving as the statewide youth ministries director (overseeing youth ministry for more than 200 churches) for my denominational fellowship for seven years and had enjoyed the privilege of having a full-time administrative assistant the whole time. We were growing and making progress. This admin had brought us to new levels of excellence. And there was no one on the horizon to replace her. But I was determined to try.

I put out feelers. I advertised. I shared publicly about my search. I needed help and I knew it. The Lord had brought along my admin who was now resigning at just the right time. Surely, if I searched hard enough, He would come through for me again with her replacement. (Christians believe stuff like that.)

When I came up empty in my search, I said to my wife, "Angela, you have to pray with me. I have GOT to find an administrative assistant to hire and soon. Work is piling up and I simply can't keep up the pace alone." Her reply caught me off-guard and, quite transparently, agitated me slightly.

She said, "Well, have you prayed about it?"

What? Of course I had prayed about it. I'm a preacher. I pray. On top of that, I'm a Christian. I pray. But apparently my prayers weren't sufficient. That's why I was enlisting her prayer support. Maybe God wanted to hear from two of us.

She continued, "Do you HAVE to hire someone? Can you do it without hiring someone?"

"Do you even know what I do?" was the question that instantly flew through my mind as we stood in the kitchen of our home. Although, I truly believe that, at that moment, the Lord saved me from my own stupidity and helped me to not say it out loud.

The only way I had led in this role was with a full-time admin serving alongside us 40+ hours per week to make everything happen at the level we had finally attained, and we had higher to climb. I didn't simply need someone as good as my previous admin. I needed an ultra superstar who could supersede that stratosphere of excellence and take us to the next level.

As if un-phased by my chagrin, Angela continued, "Well, could you hire someone part time?"

Again, words escaped me. I had recently been seriously contemplating hiring a second person part-time beyond a full-time admin just to help us excel. To think about scaling back to one part-time person seemed unthinkable, and I told Angela as much.

Apparently I had "Ask me questions I don't even want to consider the answer to" tattooed across my forehead that day, because she seemed to feel compelled to drive me right up to the brink of insanity.

Proceeding with her creative interrogation, she asked, "What about getting a couple of people here in the area to volunteer a few hours a week or whenever you have a big project?"

This was spiraling out of control. My thoughts were swimming. We went from talking about hiring a full-time assistant to hiring a part-time assistant to gathering a few local volunteers to pitch in occasionally.

And then she brought the conversation full-circle by saying, "Allen, I don't know what the answer is, but I don't think I'd rush into hiring someone just because you don't think you can handle it. Maybe there is a way to accomplish the same things differently that we haven't thought of yet. I think I'd pray about it some more and ask the Lord what the best thing to do is in this situation."

And with that, the conversation was over.

I was stunned. I was numb. I was at a loss for words, and anyone who knows me at all knows that rarely happens to me. What was I going to do? My own wife, the woman God brought alongside me as a companion and a completer, had just left me with nowhere to turn but back to God.

All I can say now is... Thank God for a great wife! And thankfully (that time) I took her advice. I went back to God with my concerns regarding what I felt like was a desperate situation. And in the midst of those conversations with the Lord, He absolutely directed my steps. I genuinely sensed deep down inside that I was to hire no one, but begin to build teams of volunteers from across our statewide fellowship to help me lead the various areas of the ministry.

Now, that may sound fine and simple on the surface, but the people I led were scattered across an entire state. Sure, the Internet existed, but video conferencing was not at all as simple & affordable as it is today. And 9 out of 10 of the people I would be asking to help already had ministry assignments in their own local churches. On top of that, many of them had to have another job outside their roles at their churches to pay their bills so that they could support their ministry habit. Which of those people could I invite to take on a whole lot more of "my work" with their already busy lives? With little-to-no pay for their work?

Beyond that, I had rarely, if ever, truly assessed the leadership capabilities of all these individuals. Who could I select? To whom could I entrust significant responsibilities? Who could I invite to lead entire areas of our organization?

Some were interested in parts of what we did, but very few in the whole of what we did. Who would love one area of the work enough to commit themselves deeply to it? Where were people's interests? What if everyone wanted to commit to one or two areas of what we did & the rest of the areas had no volunteer leaders?

But that was the plan I was given. I wonder if this was what Abram felt like when God told him to leave his home and family and go to some place that God would reveal to him when he got there. I wonder if this is what Noah felt like when God told him to build a giant boat and yet he had never seen rain? What else was I going to do though?

And so I began to dream out loud from time to time, putting out teasers with people whom I thought might become leaders of teams. I began to share that I was not going to hire anyone, and when people would ask me how I was going to accomplish everything, I would share the idea with them. If I thought they had any leadership ability at all and I sensed any openness to the concept on their part, I would invite them to consider helping to lead a team. Soon, we were signing up people to lead and serve on teams. It looked like it was all going to work out. Apparently, God really knows what He's talking about.

Five years rolled by. Some of those leaders stuck. Others did not. And while our team leaders had begun to do a fine job of taking up the slack for me not having an administrative assistant, we began to notice that some team leaders were strong in different ways. Some were great at dreaming. Others were adept at rallying the troops to accomplish tasks. Still others were gifted at seeing how ideas could be improved upon or laying out logistics. And there was still another group of leaders who were excellent when it came to checking off the to-do lists. Very few of them led in the same way, and yet they all led in some way. They accomplished their assignments somehow.

All this was a little confusing for me when I first began to recognize these differences, because I was operating under that generally-accepted, faulty assumption that all leaders who lead a team or organization are basically the same with some slight variations. I knew that we all have strengths and weaknesses. I knew that we all have to surround ourselves with people who have strengths in areas where we have weaknesses. What I didn't realize yet was that someone can wear a title, but not have been given the "D" we thought they had been given. In fact, they may not even have the "D" people think they need to get the job done.

I became acutely aware of it when I suddenly got a new boss who challenged us to re-evaluate everything we do. As I began to try to dream with various leaders who were overseeing a particular event or activity team, some did not see the concepts as clearly as I felt I did. They were looking for an assignment or looking for another team member to bring onto the team in order to handle what we were talking about.

At first, this reality was a little disconcerting for me. Again, I had some misconceptions about what it takes to be a leader. I was expecting every leader to see the big picture... the really big picture... The "Google Earth" big picture of what we were trying to accomplish and how their area fit into that big picture. I was expecting them to be brimming with ideas, dreams, and novel concepts. I was looking for wild-eyed creativity that would energize my own sometimes crazed notions about what could be.

But most of our leaders were not that at all. Sure, they could recognize a good idea. Some of them could even feed off those ideas and springboard to some other great suggestions to take an idea up a notch. Some would begin to make diagrams and lists and timetables for what would have to be done. Others would know immediately who we should invite to join the team to help us make the idea happen. And there were even those who simply wanted to know what I would like for them to do.

It did not quickly begin to crystallize for me that, when it comes to leaders... everyone gets a "D". It took several years for that to become clear. I got a "D"... You got a "D"... We all get a "D". God gives a "D" to every leader, regardless of their age, gender, or race. And that "D" is not a grade, but rather a designator of what their role on the leadership team should be... an identifier to point toward where they best fit.

You see, God does not create every leader using a Divine leadership cookie cutter. He designs us with different passions, different personalities, different purposes. And then He allows our character and overarching purpose (that's another book just sitting there waiting for me to write it) to bring us to a leadership role. There, He expects us to operate from the strength of our own personal leadership "D" and bring others alongside us to form a complete leadership team with Him at the center of it all, doing what we cannot. He does not expect for us to lead alone. Vince Lombardi said, "The man on top of the mountain didn't fall there."[2]

The truth is, you may wear a certain title as a leader and believe that you have to be able to function in specific ways. But in reality, what you need to do is to first identify your leadership designator and begin to operate in it effectively so that you know which other "D" leaders you need help from.

GIVE ME A REASON

Now, if you're like me as a reader, you're probably saying, "Okay, we get it. Different leaders on the team. Old topic. Move along." And I will, I promise. In fact, by the end of this chapter, I will give you the 5 different leadership "D" designators along with a short definition of each one. And for those of you who are quitters, you'll be tempted to stop there because you think you have it all figured out. I get it... You're smart. You're sharp. You're busy.

But I will ask you to take the whole journey with me. It is the discovery along the way of your own personal leadership journey which is really going to help solidify this concept for you. That unique, personalized discovery will help catapult you to an increased level of excellence in four ways:

• *First, it will help you in recruiting of leaders.*
Because of what I felt to be my perceived greatest weakness, I surrounded myself with only people who could fill those voids in my leadership. "Staff your weaknesses," I had heard from so many leadership gurus. I was weak in knowing how to get us from where we were to where I knew we needed to be and in checking off the to-do

list. So I always searched for those kind of leaders to help me. What I didn't realize was that I missed at least two or three other leadership "D's" on my team each time. That meant the ball often got dropped because I had recruited poorly. It wasn't that the leaders I selected to serve with me were poor leaders. I simply did not understand that they could not facilitate everything that I believed they could without having some other people on the team who could fill in the gaps where we were lacking.

Let me ask you a question... What if I told you that, by reading this book and implementing this model, you could begin identifying exactly who you need to recruit, knowing where they fit best on your team so that you can explain with clarity their role and assignments? What if you could experience more excellence and accomplish more with success?

Most leaders who are poor at recruiting are such because they don't know why they want the person they are inviting to serve with them on the team. They simply know that person is a good leader... that they like them... and/or that they think they would be a big help to the organization. But we all know that the best way to get people to buy into a vision is to clearly state it and clearly explain which part they could play in the fulfilling of that vision. The leadership "D" model will help you identify the leaders you most need AND help you place them in the proper position.

Think about how sports teams recruit for a moment. They think about what their overall style of play is as a team, what they need to do in order to defeat their opponents, and which positions they need to fill in order to achieve their goal. Then, they go after someone, either through a draft or through a trade, who plays the position they need to fill... someone who has the giftings or skill set to play that position well, in the system the team plays.

Football teams may be looking for a wide receiver who is really fast and who can blaze down the field, giving their quarterback with a strong arm a moving target. Or they still might be looking for a wide receiver, but instead one who is big and tall so that they can go up and over opposing cornerbacks for throws from their quarterback who has deadly accuracy.

If a baseball team is looking for a first baseman, they often look for someone who is left handed because it fits the position better. Or if they are looking for centerfielder, they might look for someone with a strong, accurate throw. Perhaps offense is more important to them, and they need either a slugger or a consistent hitter.

Basketball teams generally look for super tall centers to win jump balls and get rebounds, but shorter, quicker guards to move the ball down the court. And depending on the team's pace of play, they may choose one or the other to help them win.

The goal of the team determines what position needs to be filled and which qualifications or giftings a potential team player would need to bring to the table. Knowing which players you already have can make identifying the players you need to bring onto the team that much easier.

By the end of this book, you will be able to begin assessing your team, your own personal role on the team, and who you need to obtain through "draft or trade."

- *Second, sticking with the process will help you interact more effectively with your leadership team.*

What I discovered in the process of coming to this leadership "D" model is that I was often meeting with the wrong leaders to accomplish what we needed to accomplish for a task or event or project. Don't misunderstand. This is not a tiered system I'm talking about. It's not that these people were below me on the food chain.

I just didn't always have the right conversations with the right leader at the right time to keep everything moving forward properly.

Sometimes the problem was that I wanted to share vision that was new and beginning to take shape in my heart and mind. I needed to share the ideas being conceived with others who could understand what I was dreaming, pull it out of me, and inspire me to go for it. Often I was sitting down to meet with leaders who wanted a to-do list which didn't exist yet, or with someone who wanted to know the timeline and how everything would be accomplished. In the end, I often wasted time, emotional energy and money on meetings which drained me and left me feeling frustrated instead of invigorated.

If you know that feeling well, then it might be in your best interest to stick with the process I outline in this book. Save yourself a lot of time, emotional strength and money by learning how to determine which leaders you most need to meet with at which juncture in the process of completing a task, project or event.

- *Third, it will help you choose with whom to meet and when.*
Now this may sound a lot like I'm repeating what I just said, but there is a difference. The truth is, we all know that you need to meet with the whole team at times throughout the process. But most of the time, you need to meet with people who can help you be your most effective at the role you play on the leadership team.

There is an order to completing a task or project. You might have numerous events of significant value and importance to produce throughout the year. And in all of these tasks, projects and events, it is a little easier to see how all the leadership "D's" fit into place, but this principle also applies to your greater overall mission.

An organization's mission is often broad on purpose. And yet, this can put many quality leaders in a quandary about who they should spend the bulk of their meeting times with and when. Once you discover your own leadership "D", as well as helping others on your team discover theirs, you will find that you can easily determine those team members with whom you need to meet, how often and when to meet with them in the process of pursuing your overall mission.

This will probably mean that you end up meeting with some team members more than others. That's okay. All great leaders do this. Don't give into the pressure of spreading yourself thin so that everyone feels like they are getting an equal amount of your time. As leaders, we don't have the option of letting feelings run our organization. I'm not at all suggesting that you ignore people's feelings in most instances. It's a cold-hearted leader who ignores people's feelings and only cares about getting the job done at any cost. Instead, address them. When you help people on your team discover their leadership "D", it will make it easier to walk them through understanding how they best fit into the process. You will be able to value them for their specific role on the team and make them feel great about that, even if that means they meet with you less or with less regularity while others meet with you more often.

Again, this is not new. In Scripture, Aaron was often allowed close, personal access to Moses, and then Moses added Joshua to the inner circle of leadership. Even after Moses added 70 leaders, they did not all get to hang out with him all the time. That was reserved mostly for Joshua. Joshua even went into the tent of meeting with Moses to meet with God personally. Don't you think that Aaron or some of the other leaders felt a little left out at times? That wasn't Moses' fault. He was training his successor, a person with a similar leadership "D."

Jesus ministered to crowds. He sent out 70 followers at one point to represent Him. He chose twelve companions who basically stayed with Him day-in and day-out. He took three of those twelve with Him to some places and into some situations that He didn't take the rest, and one of those three was known as "the disciple whom Jesus loved." (John 20:2). How would you like to be one of those other disciples? You know, one of those whose names most people can barely remember when they are trying to list all twelve on a gameshow?

Paul said that he had no one like Timothy. How do you think that made Luke feel, the guy who also traveled with him everywhere and wrote down an account of all the great things God used Paul to accomplish?

I'm not just talking about personalities or those with whom we have the greatest connection. I'm not talking about our insecurities which can cause us to only want to meet with a limited number of people because we can't seem to grow beyond our own limits. I'm talking about the fact that great leaders identify those with whom they need to meet most, and they do so without the intent to "keep out of the loop" or hurt anyone else. They simply spend time with those they need to spend time with in order to accomplish the goal.

As you help your team identify their leadership "D" designators, you will find that you can be far more strategic in your meetings, and that you can accomplish more in those meetings.

• *And fourth, it will even help you assign tasks more productively.*
Finding the right person for the job is key. Finding the right job for the person can be an even greater challenge. Once you've recruited a leader to help you, you have to know which assignments best fit them.

This was my first initial "aha" moment in this principle becoming real to me. I realized that I had been asking the wrong things of many of the leaders on our team, and that I had to start putting the right assignments in their hands based on their leadership "D". Super-creative people don't want to be saddled with a to-do list, and task-driven leaders sometimes struggle to think outside the box.

When I began to take note of our team's individual leadership "D's," I began to see people begin to relax and enjoy their role on the team more. When they enjoyed their role more, they became more productive. That's mostly because they were being allowed to operate in the way they were designed to operate... in their leadership "D."

Operating in what they were designed for led to increased confidence in those leaders. Why? They could lead confidently because they clearly understood their role and knew they had the skill set for it. It taught them that they only had to focus on doing what they do best, and to value others on their team who had different roles. They could celebrate the differences instead of criticizing them, and when people are celebrated, they become more productive.

I'd say those are four pretty good reasons for not stopping at the end of this chapter. I don't know a leader alive who doesn't want to accomplish those four things. If you want to accomplish those things as a leader, you have to believe the leaders on your team do also.

PEGGING PEOPLE

One other danger of quitting this process at the end of this first chapter is that you will feel horrible about yourself as a person.

You may not care that you're a quitter. Or it may be that you're just not "feeling it" with this book right now. No problem. Put it down and come back to it in 3 months. That way we will both know that you're not really a quitter.

In all seriousness, there is a more legitimate and realistic danger inherent with stopping after you discover what the five leadership "D" designators are. That danger is that you could be tempted to "peg" people and look to remove people from your team without understanding the full concept and how to utilize it.

Ever pegged someone? No, I don't mean throwing hard objects at people with the intent of hurting them. The kind of pegging I'm talking about here is the kind that we do unintentionally. And yet, it can often hurt even worse.

We "peg" a person when we label them them as only being able to fit into a certain spot. We don't accept that they could change their shape, or that their shape could be designed for another spot that fits them just as well or better.

You might wrongly peg them as being a one-trick pony who doesn't fit into your circus. And as such, you could be tempted to thank them for their valuable service up to this point, but let them know that you will be freeing them up to pursue other interests or leadership roles at this time.

Oh, you wouldn't jump straight to that. You would start with disappointment in their lack of what you think they should have or be as a leader. You would look for podcasts and books and conferences which you believe could help you transform them from one type of leader to another. But eventually, frustration would set in that would drive you to ask them to step down.

That could be a tragic mistake for you as a leader. It could be a tragic mistake for your organization or business. It could even

I GOT A "D" IN LEADERSHIP

be a tragic mistake for your friendship with those individuals. That's because these people are not inept. They are not incapable. They are not disloyal or untrustworthy. They are committed leaders who want to serve on your team. It's just that they lead from a different place of strength than you, and that's actually a good thing. God may have brought them to your team because, believe it or not, you need how they lead.

Say it out loud with me right now... "I need how they lead." Don't worry about the people sitting around you who think you're a weirdo. Say it out loud again... "I need how they lead."

We tend to "peg" people when we determine in our mind that they can only do certain things because of who they are. Let's be honest with ourselves here, we do this almost imperceptibly quite often.

- *"That person is a great graphic designer... So she can only do creative things."*
- *"That person communicates well... So he can only stand on a stage and speak."*
- *"That person is great with details... So she can only be an administrator."*

"Pegging" people often causes us to limit their possibilities and overlook their fullest potential. The leaders on your team are more than a simple assignment or title. If you view them as "pegged," then you will never believe in their ability to lead. Yet they are indeed leaders... Gifted leaders.

Here is what you have to know... They *CAN* lead. They can lead well. They can lead successfully. They can be fantastic leaders... *IF* you lead them well in understanding their leadership "D" designator so that they can lead well... and give them the best opportunities to operate in that designation. That means a great deal hinges on you understanding this concept and clearly, patiently walking through it with them, doesn't it? I like to say, "It takes someone who got a 'D' in leadership to know one."

You see, nowhere in a Scripture do we find that God utilizes only one kind of leader. Instead, exactly the opposite is what we find. God chose people whose hearts were in sync with His and who were willing to lead realizing that they got a "D" in leadership. God used leaders who were big picture visionaries. He used leaders who knew how to rally the troops. He used leaders who were hands-on, get the job done people, and He used people who knew how to work with leaders with a different "D" than they had.

Let me ask you... Are you going to be that kind of leader? Are you willing to learn about your leadership "D" so that those others whom you influence can discover theirs? Are you going to release others to lead from a strength that is different from yours even if it seems a little unusual, uncomfortable or unconventional?

Well, if you are, then sit back, buckle up and hang on to your seat because this is about to be a refreshing transformation in your leadership. Just so that you don't lose heart, though, here are those promised leadership "D's" along with a brief definition of each one:

1. *Dreamers*- Those leaders who are visionaries, who see the end result from before the beginning of the process and who can state the broad goal

2. *Designers*- Those leaders who hear the vision, who are early adopters and who have amazing ideas which clarify or simplify the goal, catapulting the process forward in excellence

3. **Developers**- Those leaders who buy into the vision, who understand the goal and who can clearly delineate the action steps required to accomplish the goal
4. **Delegators**- Those leaders buy into the vision, who understand the clearly defined goal and who have the ability to rally their network of relationships to accomplish the action steps in order to accomplish the goal
5. **Doers**- Those leaders who buy into the vision, who understand the goal and who can complete all of the assigned tasks on a to-do list in order to accomplish the goal

There they are, and I have a hunch that you are already forming a strong suspicion as to which "D" you received in leadership. That's good. You'll need to know this, though... You probably have a close second with one of the other "D's" because the truth is that most of us bleed over into another area. This usually is one on either side of our "D", and it has to do with the handing off of assignments as we work together with others on our team. Additionally, you might be surprised by which "D" you really have.

And if you're not sure which "D" you have been given, don't worry. This book is about discovery. (Hey look, another "D" word! Yay me!)

In each chapter of the first section covering one of the five "D's", we will focus on the delight, the dilemma, the danger and the discipline that each of these leaders can expect to encounter as a primary leader. In the second section of the book, there is an assessment tool for you to use to more accurately define which "D" you operate from as a leader. Then, after you clearly understand the concept, we will look at how to find, attract and invite those four other "D" leaders to be a part of your team.

Once you've used this book and its model yourself, you will probably want those on your team to read this book & take the assessment themselves. The more people in your organization who really understand and embrace this approach, the more successful your team building will be.

So, let's get at it...

CHAPTER 2

DREAMERS

YOU KNOW WHAT WE SHOULD DO, DON'T YOU?

LOVE THEM OR hate them, Dreamers call us to leave the comfort of the cove & head for open waters in the hope that there might be untold riches in the lands of our discoveries if we will only go on the grand adventure with them. They are those with spyglass in hand hollering to hoist the sails and launch into the unknown.

Truth be told, we all typically think every leader ought to have this "D", and it is that misconception which creates the very problem this book is trying to solve. While there must be a visionary leader on the team for ultimate success (i.e., Steve Jobs with Apple), the leader with the ranking title or primary leadership role does *NOT* have to be a Dreamer. Still, most organizations seek out that kind of leader for their top roles, and therefore many leaders in primary roles are in fact Dreamers. This further drives the common misconception that the primary leader on a team must be a Dreamer.

The truth is that Dreamers are vitally important to the team. King Solomon, quite possibly the wisest man to ever live outside of Jesus Christ, said that without a vision people perish, or cast off restraint and run wild. It takes someone who can see a preferable future for an organization to grow, progress and become more excellent. It takes someone who can see that things need to change before anyone will ever begin to work at fixing what's broken or make improvements on what they have already achieved. It takes a Dreamer.

So why is it that we can't live with them and we can't live without them? What makes them tick? What potentially makes them a ticking time bomb? Let's take a look at these Dreamers whom we so desperately need on our team if we are going to succeed.

If you are a Dreamer, this chapter will absolutely resonate, and hopefully you will learn how you can best serve the team with your leadership "D" and without imploding. If you're not a Dreamer, perhaps you'll recognize why you need one on your team and what it will take to function together.

THE DREAMER'S DELIGHT

The Dreamer's delight is to see the needed change and share it with others. It's as if they just can't help themselves. They are visionaries.... future-casters... purveyors of opportunities.

A dreamer walks onto the scene, assesses the current situation, sees the possibilities and potential for the organization to excel to new heights of excellence and generally knows the direction the organization should go in to make progress. This is what every design consultant on a home redecorating television show is made of. Open the door of the house, invite them into a room, and before you can finish proper introductions or share what you would like their help with, they have already analyzed what is wrong in the room, how the furniture needs to be repositioned, how to change the lighting, what color scheme would work best and what pieces of decor are missing. Dreamers have an uncanny ability to scan current realities, analyze situations and envision the changes in what seems like nano-seconds compared to the rest of us. It's just what they do. They find incredible joy and fulfillment in seeing and knowing what needs to happen.

The truth is, the Dreamer's delight doesn't stop with knowing what needs to happen for the future to be bright. They also delight in telling others what they have discovered. They love to paint the rosy picture of a family room in which the family will enjoy entertaining, or increased sales which will grow the company, or more filled seats, or more lives impacted with the Good News. They are so excited about the possibilities that they can hardly constrain themselves. In fact, they are so "juiced" about what could be that they believe everyone else will be as well.

Dreamers almost enjoy finding a challenging situation, it seems. It's in those times that their antennas go up, their creativity kicks into gear and their wheels start turning. When the light bulb goes on for them with the answer of where people need to head in order to experience something greater, they are elated to let someone else know that everything is going to be alright as long as everyone take the prescribed path.

THE DREAMER'S DILEMMA

Sadly, for most Dreamers, their dilemma is that they don't know how to get to where they believe the organization is supposed to go. It is both their blessing and their curse. It is the characteristic and gift that makes them crucial to the success of the organization and yet a failure if they don't realize that they cannot do it alone.

REALITY SINKS IN

Angela and I drove two hours to meet one of our leaders and his wife for lunch to dream about one of the events we led for students. I had a couple of ideas to pitch about ways we could completely revamp the event and bring it to new levels of excellence. I had also invited Angela and this couple to come with dreams and ideas of their own which we could throw into a pot, seeing what settled to the bottom and what rose to the top.

We arrived, exchanged greetings, caught up on life, ordered and ate. As we were close to finishing our meals, I turned the discussion toward our set agenda... Dreaming. For thirty minutes, I tried to no avail to pull dreams out of everyone else after sharing mine. I couldn't understand why it wasn't working like I had planned. These were top level, committed, talented leaders. Why were dreams not bursting out of them from the seams?

Suddenly, what seemed like out of nowhere to me, Angela suggested we focus on the schedule for the event and how it could be different. When she did, it was like she threw a switch. Everything about how we were going to design and develop the best idea for the event began to flow. We sat there another two hours laying out multiple elements of that event before it finally felt too awkward to hold up that table for the waiter any longer. I mean, if we had stayed any longer, we would have had to order supper. So, we hugged (because I'm a hugger), got into our respective vehicles and drove away.

We weren't five minutes down the road after leaving that meeting, when I asked Angela what had just happened. The meeting had not gone anything like I had planned, and I couldn't put my finger on what went wrong. She replied that she felt like we were just not breaking through on the dreaming stuff and that if we could just move on to the topic of the schedule maybe we could get the ball rolling. She was right. She knows that she is not a dreamer, and she realized that the other couple were not dreamers. They didn't get the Dreamer "D". They got another "D" in leadership.

My myopia was that I am a Dreamer, and I couldn't grasp why everyone wasn't elated with my dreaming. I wanted them to dream with me. I felt like they had to see the future like I did if they were going to be top level leaders.

I was wrong. I didn't need more dreamers sitting at the table with me. I needed people gifted with the other four leadership "D's" to come alongside me and help me figure out exactly how we were going to get where I sensed we needed to go.

You see, the dilemma for a Dreamer is that they see the end from the beginning. That is, they see where the organization is now... what it's current condition is within its environment. The good, the bad, and the ugly. They see it all. They see clearly what the organization could look like... would look like... should look like. The great, the victorious, and the beautiful. And ten out of ten times, a Dreamer sees a different potential reality for the organization compared to its current condition. No matter how much is accomplished or attained, the Dreamer always sees the potential for more, for greater, for expansion, for growth.

This is a dilemma for the Dreamer because not everyone else on the team sees the current condition, nor the need to change. Many like the status quo and are quite content to keep things the same. Why rock the boat?

So, when the Dreamer tries to share the dreams in their heart and mind, others don't always receive it or even understand it. Then the Dreamer sets those people aside for their apparent lack of foresight and looks for other leaders whom he/she believes will "get it" and dream with them. But too often, the Dreamer is the only Dreamer in the room, and other leaders aren't sure how to respond to that person's dreams.

That is the juncture when the dilemma for the Dreamer can actually turn into their danger if it isn't headed off at the pass.

THE DREAMER'S DANGER

The inherent danger for the Dreamer is thinking that everyone else is also a dreamer & sharing the dream with the wrong people.

HERE COMES THE DREAMER

Joseph (of Old Testament fame in Scripture) had no clue what he was getting himself into when he boldly shared his God-given dreams with his family. Most of us knock him for not using wisdom. We say he should have just kept his dreams to himself, and perhaps he could have stayed out of trouble.

But was that really true? Can a Dreamer really keep it bottled up inside? I'm not so sure they can. I say that because I am a confessed Dreamer. That's the primary "D" I believe I got in leadership. I feel Joseph's struggle. When you're a Dreamer, especially a Dreamer in the role of primary leader, you believe everyone else needs to, and wants to, hear how much better things could actually be. So, I don't fault Joseph too much.

Joseph came from a line of men who talked with God about big subjects. He was a fourth generation son of God's promise. He had grown up hearing from his dad and his granddad how amazing his family's life was going to be.

On top of that, he was his dad's favorite. It was obvious. The Armani-like tailoring on his multi-colored, bold coat made him stand out among his otherwise drably clothed brothers. Jacob, Joseph's dad, apparently couldn't help himself. He just had to let everyone know how special that boy was to him.

So, perhaps it came as no shock to Joseph when he had those dreams in which he was the center of attention and the rest of the family was submitting to his leadership. Maybe he thought to himself, "Well would you look at that... God is confirming what Dad has said about me. Looks like I really *AM* destined for greatness and there is no way around it. That's pretty cool!"

Who wouldn't want to tell those closest to you what you see about the future? I'll tell you who... People who didn't get the Dreamer "D" from God to help them lead. People who are not Dreamers are generally not interested in buying whatever brand of a changed future you're trying to sell. They don't necessarily believe that things can get better. Even if things can get better, they aren't sure it's worth all the effort. And they sure don't believe that *YOU* have all the right answers about how things should be.

Thus the response of Joseph's brothers of, "Here comes the dreamer!" (Genesis 37:19). They had heard enough of his dreams. They did not look forward to a future that preferred him... again. They simply could not see a situation in which things would be so different that they would be okay with him being the authority in their lives.

Now granted, most people on your team will not oppose you so vehemently that they want to do you bodily harm. But make no mistake, those on your team who are not Dreamers will not be nearly as interested in your dreams as you are.

In truth, the danger for a Dreamer in leading is two-fold:

1) Arrogance as a leader. Arrogance happens when you think that you have all the answers as a leader and that, because no one else cares about your dreams as much as you do, no one else understands or can be involved in the process. For Dreamers, it is difficult to grasp that what they see so easily and so fully, very few others seem to see at all. To a Dreamer, the challenges of today and the potential for a changed tomorrow are as plain as the proverbially nose on your face. So, when they share a dream (aka, cast vision) and no one bites, they are confused and frustrated. They wonder how no one else can understand what is so clear to them. When the mislabeled naysayers begin to ask the "How?" and "Why?" kind of questions, a Dreamer begins to feel like people are not interested, just opposed to the dream. They can even begin to have a sense of superiority, believing they simply know better than everyone else what must be done.

Sadly, I've been there. I told you that the "D" I got in leadership is the Dreamer "D." I could point to countless times I've tried to share with teams, a student body, friends or even family what I see as the current unacceptable situation and what the acceptable different future situation could be, only to find myself met with hesitation, skepticism or outright opposition.

In those moments, there are some wrong decisions which are easily made. A Dreamer could be tempted to say things like, "No one else gets this like I do," or, "Fine, I won't share my dreams anymore. I'll just keep them to myself." It would seem to make sense that this might actually work, but the problem is that a Dreamer was designed to dream. He/She doesn't quit seeing current conditions and future potential. So this response leads to frustration as a leader. It also leads to a lone wolf mentality. Neither of these attitudes is helpful or productive at making the dream become a reality.

A Dreamer who feels rebuffed may be tempted to think more of themselves than is appropriate and say something like, "I can handle it alone." They begin to feel as if no one understands, or that no one cares about the dream. They isolate themselves in an attempt to insulate themselves. They need the team, but arrogance prevents them from seeing that the dream may need tweaking or adjusting. They fail to see that they truly need others to make sure the dream becomes reality. Yet, no one wants to join the team led by an arrogant jerk.

2)   *Naïvety as a leader.* Naïvety comes into play by sharing your dreams carelessly as a leader. Like Joseph in the account I shared earlier, Dreamers are often genuinely excited about what they are realizing. They are excited about fulfilling their purpose. That excitement can short-circuit their effectiveness if they are not careful.

Naïvety as a Dreamer comes disguised as trying to bring people to the team to help the dream become reality. The Dreamer expects that sharing the dream with people will cause them to want to jump on the train of change and go where the train takes them. Often though, sharing the dream in an unwise manner has the opposite effect and drives people away from the dream.

Dreamers can injure their cause and derail the dream if they naïvely share the dream with the wrong people or at the wrong time. Both of these mistakes in sharing the dream can be dream-crushers at worst and deal-delayers at best.

The naïve Dreamer will struggle to build a team from lack of wisdom. People will think that leader is just "going off half-cocked," that the leader has not really thought everything through adequately.

THE DREAMER'S DISCIPLINE

What's a Dreamer to do? Identify the problem and discipline themselves to solve it. Sounds easy, right? Unless you're having incredible dreams that drive everyone around you nuts.

The truth is, Dreamers often feel like they can't help but share the dreams with everyone. They are geeked out of their minds to know that there are answers to questions or solutions to problems and that they have those answers or solutions. They assume that when everyone in the organization finally realizes that something has to change, then certainly everyone in the organization will be thrilled that someone has those answers or solutions.

What most Dreamers fail to grasp is that every one of the other four leadership "D" leaders might feel just as geeked out about the dream... if they could get their questions answered about the why and the how and the who and the what. It's not like Dreamers don't know those things will have to come at some point. They just want to feel like everyone is on-board with them before they get to those parts.

Usually, the issue for Dreamers comes down to the communication of the dreams... getting what is inside of them, outside. There are four steps in the process of disciplining themselves for greater effectiveness:

1) Learn. When we talk about Dreamers needing to learn, we mean learning when to share the dream and when to just keep the dream between themselves and God.

Timing is crucial for a Dreamer. Not every dream should be shared immediately because not every dream is a good dream. Not every dream is for that moment. Some dreams are just your own neat ideas, but are not good ideas for the organization. Some dreams are great for the organization, but are for a later time.

Keep the dream to yourself for a short while. Write it down. Mull it over. Pray about it. You may take anywhere from a few days for a smaller dream to months for a grander dream. Just give it some time before you say anything about it. Let it simmer. In South Louisiana, they say a really good gumbo is cooked "low and slow." A great dream is processed the same way in our hearts and minds... quietly, and over time.

Then, as you determine it is the right dream and it is the right time, begin to share the dream slowly. Be strategic about whom you share the dream with, and how much of it you share. There is no rule book anywhere that says you have to send out an all points bulletin to the entire organization unloading a dream thirty seconds after the idea pops in your head.

2. Look. Look for others with whom you can dream safely. In order for you to be effective in leading, you will have to find two other types of people:

Find other Dreamers to dream with. They may or may not have an official role on your team. They may or may not even work within your organization. They might be friends or counterparts in another organization. Or they may be people within your own organization with whom you just simply never considered dreaming before. But finding those other Dreamers will help you discover a release valve that will help you lead to your fullest potential, without wrecking the organization in the process.

You need to identify some fellow Dreamers with whom you can initially share ideas. These may not even be people that are added to the team in some specific role. They may be friends or mentors. Or if they are in the organization, they could even be subordinates. But the leadership "D" they got is obviously the Dreamer "D".

Dreamers need other dreamers with whom they can share their dreams. They need people who get what it's like to see the end result without knowing the path to get there. They need others who can celebrate the joy of knowing a direction without having a completed map of how to get to the destination. They need to surround themselves initially with people who cheer their ingenuity and creativity, their boldness and their daring.

Truth be told, it often takes a Dreamer to understand and celebrate a Dreamer. So, before launching that incredible vision to the entire team and beginning the process of working toward it, a Dreamer would do well to invite a few other Dreamer friends to coffee where he or she can holler "Eureka," and have those friends holler "Hoorah" in response.

The other type person to look for with whom you can share your dreams can be found as you take the next step...

3. *Lean.* Lean toward the right "next" people on the team who you know can accept the vision.

Lean toward Designers to pour fuel on the fire of your dream. We will talk about this more in depth in the next chapter, but here's a teaser to whet your appetite. While these people are not the kind to immediately see a preferred future, they do grab hold of a vision fairly quickly and have great ideas to nudge it forward, giving it momentum.

4. Lead. Surround yourself with the right team members to get the vision accomplished.

Dreamers need to find a way to share the vision of what they perceive to be a better future in which non-dreamers can initially accept it before they begin to process it.

The story of Joseph in the Old Testament is an excellent example of a dreamer who shared his vision of what he thought was a potentially better future, but in such a way that those he shared it with couldn't accept it initially. So because they couldn't accept it initially, they didn't accept it for years until it was actually forced upon them due to their dire situation.

And sadly, many Dreamers today suffer the same fate as Joseph... having people oppose them and their leadership... because they fail to find a way to share the vision they have for a potentially better future in a manner which those who are not Dreamers can initially accept so that they can begin to process it.

So, in order for Dreamers to be most effective, they have to be able to share the vision for change in a way others can accept. This involves taking a few practical steps. These steps are the feet to the four principles of the Dreamer's Discipline listed above.

And if you have been blessed with the Dreamer "D", you'll probably want to get out a sticky note or an index card to write these on and then put it where you can read them regularly-- or better yet, make the list a picture and save it as the lock screen on your phone-- because these are going to save you a lot of heartache...

1) *Hold that dream.* Write it down. (Read Habakkuk 2:2-3 in the Bible). Give it time before you share it.
2) *Get together with your pre-screened, pre-selected Dreamer-friends... and let it all out.*
3) *Think of any questions others might ask about this vision for change, and add the answers to those questions into your presentation plan.*
4) *Share your dream with one or two people on your team who are close to you and believe in you.* Say something like, "If I were to tell you that I think we could _____, how do you think other people on our team would feel about that, and why?"
5) *Restrain yourself from sharing the whole vision all at once with the whole team.* Everyone on the team is not ready for it yet. Let them come along at their own pace.
6) *Begin to build a team to include the other four leadership "D's" so that you can actually achieve what is in your heart.*

NOTE: One last suggestion for Dreamers... Being a Dreamer is not an excuse to be lazy. The other four leaders, especially the Doers, are not going to appreciate your leadership "D" contribution if you don't get in there and hustle with them. So dream for sure, and then help the others make the dream come alive.

Dreamers... you've gotta love them. No, seriously, you've got to love them. You've got to believe that there is a perfect place for them on the team in order to make a powerful difference.

We need Dreamers. Dreamers make "new" possible. Dreamers innovate and help solve crucial problems. Dreamers are optimists... those who believe in the impossible becoming possible. Dreamers (with a right heart) believe life can be better and genuinely want others to experience that better life.

If you're not a Dreamer, please don't misinterpret what you just read. I did not say they are the best leaders, or even perfect leaders. I simply said that people who are Dreamers have one of the five valuable leadership "D's" we all need for our teams to function at their highest capacity.

If you're not a Dreamer, don't worry. Your chapter is for sure coming up soon. Keep reading. You're going to build a great team!

CHAPTER 3

DESIGNERS

YOU KNOW WHAT WE COULD DO, DON'T YOU?

OVER THE YEARS, I've worked with a number of graphic designers on everything from promotional materials and products... to videos... to websites and apps... to branding and logos... and too many t-shirts to count. At first, I felt bad to say something to them if I didn't particularly care for a design they created for me.

But over the years, I became friends with some designers and discovered that what they truly want is to help pull out of me what I really have in my mind and get it out into a working format. They want to help the dream become a reality. To them, me telling them that what they designed was not exactly what I had in mind was not an insult. It was a way for them to hone down on what I was really looking for. They wanted to give me a product that reflected what I had envisioned. So they began throwing out ideas to see if they were understanding the vision I was casting.

That is the heart of those who have the Designer leadership "D." They are those who pull out of a Dreamer what that Dreamer wants to see become reality. As stated earlier, they are those leaders who hear the vision, who are early adopters and who have amazing ideas which clarify or simplify the goal, catapulting the process forward.

If you are a person who gets excited when they hear a vision for a better future, and suddenly ideas start flooding into your mind as to how that vision can be either simplified or escalated into greatness, then you just might have the Designer "D" in leadership. If that is the case for you, then you are going to need to focus on the following...

THE DESIGNER'S DELIGHT

A commercial by a major brand plumbing product company features a couple walking into an architect's prestigious office. As they sit down, the wife pulls a beautiful faucet out of her large purse and sets it on the architect's desk. Then the husband says, "Design us a house around this." To which, the architect sits back in his chair and smiles.

If you have the Designer "D," you probably smiled reading that previous paragraph. You get it. You know what it's like for someone to share their dream with you and ask for your help. And you enjoy delivering ideas for possibilities.

Designers pull weeds for Dreamers. They love asking the questions which will drill down on what is important and what is irrelevant. They start digging around to see what is beautiful about the dream and what is in the way. They both expand the possibilities and narrow the focus.

Designers carry the keys to help Dreamers put into words and pictures what is seemingly locked inside the Dreamers' heads and hearts. And they find great pleasure in being able to hear a vision and translate it into language that others on the team can accept.

If Dreamers are the vision-casters for the leadership team, then I would say that Designers are the "sloganeers." They put a handle on what the Dreamers are trying to communicate. They are able to hear the vision, accept the vision, help refine the vision, and set the Dreamer up to share the vision in a powerful, compelling way.

Additionally, Designers are the "elevators." They have the ability to raise the dream to a whole new level of excellence with their ideas. They springboard off a Dreamer's vision like an Olympic athlete setting up for the dive of their life.

My wife, Angela, is one of the greatest Designer "D" leaders I know. My problem is that far too often I have waited too late to bring her into the process on a dream, only to discover she could have helped me so much more if I had just invited her into it earlier.

Those times when I have waited too late to include her and she says, "Oh, man! You know what you could have done to make this better, don't you," I usually end up frustrated and kicking myself. It's like she just "gets it" and has great ideas to take the dream from an idea to a great possibility.

On the other hand, when I have included her early enough in the process, she kicks into gear Googling and finding stuff on Amazon or Pinterest which help me begin to sharpen the focus of the dream. It's not just because we're married. I've seen her do the same thing with other Dreamers over the years.

Designers' eyes light up when they hear a vision which has marinated sufficiently in the Dreamer and is presented in such a way by the Dreamer that they express a desire for help. That's what Designers live for. They want to come alongside a Dreamer and take those dreams to the next level.

Often, the Designer gets confused for a Dreamer because it seems like they are the idea people. In a sense they are, but the reality is that they simply heard a powerful dream shared well by an excellent Dreamer, and their wheels of Designing began to roll.

A Designer finds their delight in being invited into the heart and mind of the Dreamer... being allowed to excavate the vision and mine out the gem which will eventually be presented to the world... being able to shape it and polish it some... and then putting it back in the hand of the Dreamer to share with the rest of the team.

THE DESIGNER'S DILEMMA

Chester Cheetah says, "It ain't easy bein' cheesy." And so it is that the Designer also has their own dilemma... Namely, they can't help if they aren't included in the process. And even more accurately, if they are not included at the proper time in the process from dream to reality. The Designer's dilemma can be two-fold:

First dilemma. If you are not the primary leader and you are a Designer, you sometimes have no choice about when you are invited into the process.

Designers function at their best on the front end of any dream. They do well when a Dreamer has let a dream simmer a little, shared it with a few other close Dreamers, and is ready to test the waters with a trusted individual on their team. Designers do their best work when they are some of the first to hear an idea and are given some time to beat it around before it is shared with others.

The further along in the process they are brought into the process, the less they are able to help. Time crunches don't work for them. And this creates a sense of frustration in them. They think to themselves that they would have been able to help if there were more time, or if resources had been allocated differently. Additionally, once the wheels are in motion on the project of transforming a vision/dream into reality, it is often difficult to back up at go at it differently just because a Designer came up with a better idea half-way through the process.

No one likes to be frustrated. And when the Designer is brought into the process too late, it creates frustration for not only the Designer, but also for the Dreamer and the Developer. Again, this concept is not only about staffing your weaknesses. It's about bringing the right team members to the table at the right point in the process.

Second dilemma. If you are the primary leader and you have the Designer leadership "D," then you may find yourself lacking the initial vision formation which some other leaders expect. You may have been given an assignment or a title because your boss likes you... or because your resume is impressive... or because you have made significant contributions to previous projects. You make have even been handed a leadership role because you are "an idea person" in the mind of your supervisor. Yet you realize that you don't fit the general Dreamer mold many think of when they think of a team leader.

Suddenly, you may find yourself being called upon to pitch some ideas or share your heart about where you want to see this particular division or project go. You may be asked to lead in the common way of thinking about leaders. And you may be drawing a blank. It's okay. Take a deep breath.

There's a Dreamer out there who can help you. You just need to find them and bring them onto your team. I'm not saying that you should tell your boss, "I've got nothing." And I don't believe you have to tell them that you are not the right person for the job. You probably are if they picked you, but perhaps saying, "Let me get back to you on that because I want to work through a couple things with someone else first and bring you the best ideas possible," wouldn't be out of line.

THE DESIGNER'S DANGER

As with each of the Leadership "D's," there is an inherent danger for the Designer which, if not recognized and avoided, can wreck the possibility of success in leading. That danger for the Designer is… too much, too fast. And it plays out in two similar, but slightly different ways.

1) *"Too much, too fast" can happen in the form of overwhelming the Dreamer.* Dreamers who have learned to be cautious about sharing the vision for a better future with too many people will be excited to find someone who gets the vision… who accepts the vision… who wants to engage in the vision. As they experience this with a Designer, they will begin to open the floodgates of the dream.

Upon hearing the incredible vision the Dreamer shares, ideas will begin filling the brain of the Designer like kernels of corn in a hot air popper beginning to pop and fill their reservoir till they spill out into a bowl. Initially, this is exciting and enjoyable for both the Dreamer and the Designer. But soon after the first few kernel ideas have popped out, the Dreamer can begin to put the brakes on.

Why? Quite simply because the Dreamer is a Dreamer. They recognize that things could be better than they are now, and they see a finished product in their mind's eye. The Designer's ideas begin to add great value and focus to the vision. Usually, the first few ideas from the Designer come slowly... like those popcorn kernels. This gives the Dreamer time to process them, deciding which ones stick or which ones help propel the vision forward. But like the popcorn kernels, once the heat is generated and some start popping, it seems like a flood soon follows. The same is true with the Designer's ideas. Soon they can kick out so many ideas that the Dreamer's "bowl" (mind) is full to overflowing. And the Dreamer cannot handle too many ideas too quickly.

Why not? Quite simply because the Dreamer is a Dreamer. They are not a Developer... or a Delegator... or a Doer. So they see an end product of a better future and have some great ideas on how to take it to an even higher level of excellence, but they don't know how to accomplish it. Soon, they are swimming in a sea of popcorn ideas with no idea of how all those ideas can be accomplished, who to get to help, or what the task list is going to look like to know when it is finished.

I love sitting in a room of leaders, sharing vision with them, and then hearing the first several popcorn kernel ideas start to emerge. I also hate sitting in that same room, with that same group of leaders, and having so many good ideas that I don't know where to start or how to get any of them accomplished so that the dream in my heart can become a reality.

And so the Designer overwhelms the Dreamer, and the Dreamer pulls away. It's probably fear that causes them to pull away. It's not that they don't love the ideas. It's just that they cannot fathom how to pull it all together, and most of the time, the Designer doesn't know all those details either. They just know that their ideas will improve the vision. So, the Designer must be self-aware of the fact that they have the ability to overwhelm a Dreamer and actually shut down a dream. This all occurs because it was too much, too fast.

2) *"Too much, too fast" occurs is when it causes the Dreamer to feel like the dream is being hijacked.* Hijacked... you know, taken over.

In all the excitement of hearing the vision for a better future and allowing the ideas of how to clean up or escalate that vision to flow out of themselves, the Designer can actually begin to create a sense that they have taken the vision away from the Dreamer, transforming it into their own vision, their own agenda, their idea.

Suddenly, a Dreamer feels like the stagecoach of their leadership just got held-up at gunpoint... like they were made to get out and walk while the Designer-robber drives off with their vision for a better future. It's bad enough for the Dreamer that they can see the end result in their mind's eye but don't know how to accomplish it. It's even more frustrating when someone else seems to be a great idea person.

For a Dreamer, this can deal a blow to their self-esteem. It probably shouldn't, but hey, we're all human. And for a Dreamer who feels like their "one thing" is being able to point in the direction an organization should go... or paint a picture for the whole team of how a project could make a difference, when a Designer begins clarifying the vision and coming up with a ton of ideas, people can be drawn to that person's leadership instead of the Dreamer.

It makes sense because it's the next step to moving the vision forward. Developers and Delegators need to be brought on-board so they draw up a real idea, a real plan. They connect more with the Designer. And a dangerous schism develops between the Dreamer and the Designer which could slow down or halt progress on a dream which really needs to become reality.

THE DESIGNER'S DISCIPLINE

Those dangers sound tragic for personal relationships within a work environment, as well as for the work itself. So, how do you avoid these dangers if you are a Designer?

The Designer's discipline can be applied in two different leadership-role scenarios:

First, if you are **not** the primary leader:

1) *Let the Dreamer know you are available to serve and that you are only interested in helping in the process.* Clearly define what you see your role as being in the leadership process. Take away any opportunity for the Dreamer to see you as a threat to their role.

2) *Learn how much the Dreamer can accept from you.* This is a fine line to walk. Dreamers love to hear ideas about their vision, and drill down on clarifying it. Truthfully, this one may take some trial and error to actually learn. It can vary from Dreamer to Dreamer. And it can vary from vision to vision with the same Dreamer. Nothing says you can't simply ask the Dreamer if you're overwhelming them with ideas or "pulling weeds." Try that throughout the process and soon you will pick up on how much or how little they can accept.

3) Discover how you can help move the ball forward from the Dreamer to the Developer. As a Designer, you are a "hinge-pin." You are the connector between the vision being expressed and the vision beginning to be workable. Inquire openly of the Dreamer as to how they think you can best help them express the vision to the right people on the team who can take action to bring it about. Don't be insecure if they cut you out of the process at that point. They may prefer to do all the communicating. That's okay. It's what they're wired for usually, and they mean no harm by it. They're just excited about the vision.

Some, however, will want you to be in meetings and add excitement. Others may truly delegate sharing the vision in certain settings. Whatever the case, you're part of the team, and you simply need to do your part as asked to do so.

The second way in which the Designer's discipline can be applied comes into play if you **are** the primary leader:

1) Find a Dreamer and invite them to help you succeed. If you are the primary leader, but not a Dreamer, then you probably were assigned that role because someone believes you to be a Dreamer. That's okay... as long as you don't attempt to be a Dreamer. Just find someone on your team... or recruit someone onto your team (either officially or unofficially)... who is a Dreamer. Explain to them your assignment, give them the facts they need, and cut them loose to dream. Then, have them share the dream with you and begin to work your own personal Designer magic.

NOTE: We will discuss how to discover and recruit other "D" leaders for your team in Chapter 8. So don't panic if you don't know how to do this just yet.

2) Know when to say, "When." While sharing too many de-sign ideas and honing down the vision too much can drive a Dreamer nuts, at least they can tell you when it is getting to be a little too much. However, if you are the primary leader, then it is possible that you might become enthralled in all of the designing ideas and get bogged down in the process. Having a deadline and and a timeline to meet that deadline will help. Whatever the case, common sense restraint is the name of the game here.

3) Write it all down. Ideas are wonderful... and elusive... things. While you will initially choose some ideas to help drill down on the vision or elevate its excellence, others will be set aside. Yet sometimes, ideas initially deemed incredible end up being un-realistic or unachievable. If you have written down all the ideas initially, you will have a pool to go back and draw from. And sometimes an idea which did not work for one dream or project will be just what is needed for a different dream or project. If you have ideas written down, you can go back to the list and grab that idea. If you don't write the ideas down, you may or may not remember it when you need it.

Designers... They bring spice to leadership life. They ask, imag-ine and investigate. Designers clarify the vision and elevate its excellence far beyond what any of the rest of us can accomplish. Designers remind us that even great dreams can be improved upon. Designers are early adopters... believers in the both the dream and the Dreamer. Designers set up a dream to be handed off to the rest of the team.

Think about this... By simply adding one more person be-yond yourself, you have already built a team. You have pressed past the idea that you can accomplish everything alone. You are on your way to becoming more successful than you ever dreamed. Your team is not complete, though. It is still somewhat limited in its abilities to reach the fullest potential. Keep reading, and let's see who else we can add to this team for greater effectiveness and deeper impact.

CHAPTER 4

DEVELOPERS

YOU KNOW WHAT THIS WILL REQUIRE, DON'T YOU?

I LOVE TO watch those cooking shows on television. You know, the ones where they give the cooks certain ingredients to use, a theme or a style of dish, and a time limit within which the dish has to be finished and presented. Then judges taste the food and critique each cook's dish. After that, someone gets cut from the competition and the remaining cooks advance to the next round until finally only one cook is left standing and is crowned the champion in that particular type of cooking.

I suppose I love to watch those shows because I am mesmerized by people's ability to cook. You would be more likely to find me on one of those shows which features people who are completely inept at cooking. I mean, I can plate food well. I also like to eat good food. It's just that I don't understand HOW to cook. I don't know which kitchen tools will help me get the food made. I don't know which ingredients can be combined to work well together. I wonder about the difference between blending and mixing, softening and melting, sautéing and simmering. It's the process which bamboozles me.

Quite honestly, I watch in amazement as Angela whips out meals made from scratch on a daily basis. She doesn't even always use a recipe. What?! Then there are those people on the cooking shows who often have to come up with an idea in less than 30 seconds, grab the supplies, utensils and cookware they need, and are off to the races.

It's because good cooks get the process. They know what tools are going to be required. They know in what order steps have to be done for things to turn out right. They know at which temperatures certain foods should be cooked... and for how long. They understand how to time out the cooking so that foods finish at close to the same time... or in the order they will be needed to complete the dish. They grasp process.

This is the heart of those leaders who got the leadership "D" of being Developers. Developers say to the team, "You know what we have to do if you want to accomplish that vision, don't you?" To which most of the rest of the team replies, "No, what?"

That's precisely why we all need Developers on our team. They are the folks who get process. They are the ones who really geek out over the order things need to be done in, the list of tools which will be needed and building a timeline to get it all done by the deadline.

———⊗⊗⊗———

Recently, I was at a party with a number of friends. The party had moved outside around the fire pit, and I was headed that way when a couple about my age stopped to talk. We had not seen each other much for awhile and began to catch up.

Our conversation somehow turned to the topic of writing and I mentioned that I was working on the first book... this book... of what I believe will be at least eight to ten books I will write in my lifetime. The husband asked me what the book would be about, and so I began to lay out the premise of this book in general.

When I got to the part about Developers, his eyes lit up and he began shaking his head. His eyes met with his wife's, and they just grinned. She completely agreed that I had just described his passion to a "T." (She could have said to a "D" to fit in with the book, but I cut her some slack.)

Interestingly enough, this man's job involves a ton of process. And even when he does something fun, like setting up his outdoor Christmas decor at his house, for him it's all about the process.

That's a Developer, and if you're a Developer, then this chapter is for you. If you're not a Developer, I'd like to suggest that you dive into this chapter also because you need to understand them and why you need them on your team.

And so with that, let's get cooking...

THE DEVELOPER'S DELIGHT

Developers delight in the details. Details may be mundane for some, but for these leaders the details are what makes the world go round. The live by lists and charts and clocks and calendars, all the while whistling while they work.

Typically, those who are Dreamers and Designers come up with big picture ideas, but have no way of bringing those ideas into reality because they lack the knowledge of what the process would look like. They get stumped. Delegators and Doers are waiting for someone to hand them the timeline and task list.

Developers bring the team together in a way that few can. The moment they hear a clearly defined vision and those big ideas which elevate its excellence, their minds kick into gear... their wheels begin to turn... and their hearts begin to race. Nothing brings a Developer more joy than to know there is a dream which needs developing. Legal pads, sticky notes, spreadsheet software and white boards were most likely all created for Developers at some point. (Truth be told, they were probably made as a result of Developers as well.)

Math teachers... military strategists... general contractors... mechanical engineers... They're all Developers. They love to solve a problem or lay out a plan. It's how they find their fulfillment.

I love fishing. Not big saltwater fishing with massive rods and reels. I wouldn't say I'm even a bass fisherman, although I don't mind hooking a lunker occasionally. No, I enjoy catching bream and white perch (aka, crappie) on light tackle. I love using a jig pole with a cork. Toss the bait out there, let it sink, and watch the bobber. Those little bream will usually nibble around at it, but let a decent-sized bream or white perch grab that bait, and down goes the cork! There really is no feeling quite like it in life.

That is, unless you watch a Developer in action at a meeting with the team... Just let a Dreamer and a Designer come to the table with their team and pitch what the finished product of a vision will look like, and before they know it... BAM! Down goes the cork as the Developer takes off making lists of what will have to be accomplished. Then they start prioritizing, and scheduling. They begin reeling off items which will need to be secured or purchased like a white perch zinging out the line from an ultra-light spinning reel. It truly is a thing of beauty to behold.

Give a Developer a problem to solve and they will light up. Give them a deadline, and they'll give you a timeline. Give them a product, and they'll give you a purchase order for all the supplies which will be needed. Give them a project, and they'll give you a punch-list of all the steps in the process. And the funny thing is, they will have the time of their lives putting it all together for you.

Developers bring hope to Dreamers and help to Designers. What began as a possibility with the Dreamer and grew to having potential with the Designer becomes a probability when put into the hands of those who have the Developer "D." Putting together a plan for success brings joy to their work. And it also brings joy to the team.

THE DEVELOPER'S DILEMMA

Now, while the Developer delights in helping build the process for the Dream to be accomplished, and are so amazing at it, they also have their own dilemma...

Perfectionism.

In the 1800's, French novelist Gustave Flaubert was attributed with the saying "God is in the details." The saying means that God is interested in all the little details of life, and if we want to do our work with excellence, then we should also pay very close attention to the details of that work. This is true. Science bears out from the vastness of space to the microscopic level of DNA that God is indeed interested in the details. Details make a difference. This is what motivates Developers.

That saying from Flaubert spawned and morphed into another similar saying by German philosopher, Friedrich Nietzsche, in the later 1800's... "the devil is in the details," meaning that it is important to pay attention to all those details because, if you don't and you miss one, there will be problems. Even though I don't agree with the "demon around every corner" philosophy in life, it is true that not paying attention to details can lead to some pretty big issues later on in a project.

So, why would this be a dilemma for a Developer? Simple, because they believe the details are so crucial to the success of any project, they try to uncover every detail and solve every little problem... sometimes seeing problems where there are none, or trying so hard to make sure that they don't miss any detail at all, that they fail to give the team a workable plan.

Dreamers and Designers bring ideas to the table and need the help of Developers to come up with a plan in order to see the vision become reality. And Delegators and Doers are waiting on the other side of Developers to put the plan into motion in order to complete the dream. The forward propulsion of the project depends on the timeline and task list coming from the Developers in a timely manner. But fearing that they may miss something, Developers may want to go over everything one more time just to make sure. They may even fall into the trap of digging so deep down into details that they overthink minute details which would be common sense to the team members who would be tackling the tasks.

As the Developer pursues excellence and makes sure they can give the team what it needs in the way of plans, timelines, task lists, supply lists, etc., it is possible for them to feel trapped. Like Moses and the Israelites being trapped between the Red Sea in front of them and Pharaoh's army approaching behind them, the Developer can feel a sense of being trapped between needing to cover as many details as possible in front of them and being chased by not missing any mission-critical details behind them.

The fear? Perfectionism. Striking that perfect balance of covering all the right details while not adding too many details. Walking a tightrope or maneuvering on a balance beam in the Olympics might not be any different. One slip-up one way or the other might throw everything off. This can cause some Developers to doubt their God-given abilities and freeze up in the midst of a project. Or if they simply give in to their gifted-ness too much, it can complicate the process for the rest of the team.

This is the role of the Developer. And though they are built to be able to handle it... dare I say, even enjoy it... It is a balancing act they must learn to walk carefully if they are to accomplish all they are capable of if the team is to succeed. And succeed they will if they can simply avoid the following dangers which could befall them in their efforts...

THE DEVELOPER'S DANGER

Danger is not usually the first word we think of when we think of the bean-counters... the pencil-pushers... the software engineers... the schedulers. It would seem that Developers are free from dangers. Yet, the opposite is true.

It is because we underestimate the dangers for those with the Developer leadership "D," that their danger could be just as damaging to their role on the team. The danger for Developers fall into three main components:

1) *Getting bogged down in the minutiae.* Because what Developers do is details, they tend toward the "fine-toothed

comb" model of digging deep into a project in order to make sure they don't miss anything. This is great because it helps the team not miss much. But at some point, the details get so small that is is a little bit overkill.

For example, if the team is going to need to design a black logo on a white background for someone, the Developer might determine that the graphic artist will need white paper and black ink to print out some proposals. That would be sufficient. Let those who will do the ordering determine what they will order. If instead, the Developer begins to specify that the team needs to order a ream of 8.5" X 11" 24-lb white paper with a rating of 92-95 brightness made from recycled paper on a particular website using a specific discount code during a certain week of the month when that company runs a particular sale, that *MAY* be a little too much detail.

What the team needs from the Developer is how many man-hours the project will take... not when bathroom breaks are allowed. What they need from the Developer is how much space it will take to lay out the design they are wanting to build... not how how to clean up the wood shavings after they cut wood. What they need from the Developer is who to contact to reserve booth space at the local fair to get their product revealed to the public... not the distance from that booth space to the ferris wheel and the food trucks.

Minutiae. It's like quicksand for a Developer. The more you struggle to get out, the deeper you can sink.

2) Boring people with the details and costing the momentum of the dream. Sadly, the work of the Developer can be one of the least-recognized and most under-appreciated parts of the process. So sadly, the Developer can be one of the unsung heroes of any team.

The reason? Developers... and their contribution to the team... are often misunderstood due to this one element of danger. When they geek out on, and start talking non-stop about, the details of a project, most people tune out. Dreamers want to know if the dream can become reality. Designers want to know if their ideas can be incorporated into the process to make the dream a better reality. Delegators want to know how many people will be needed and in what areas so that they can build and expand the team to make the dream a reality. Doers simply want a punch-list to start working on.

Details become the detriment of the Developer if they talk too much about them.

I once worked in a job with a Developer on the team who could grind parts of meetings to a complete standstill as they asked questions about every little detail of a project. All those questions needed to be answered for sure, but most of us did not need to be in on the conversation. We just needed to know the highlights and our assignments. We were grateful for that person's contribution to the effectiveness of the team. We just wanted to get back to working on the projects a little sooner.

Not everyone can appreciate the details. Not everyone can even accept that details are necessary. (Those people desperately need a Developer on their team more than they know.). So it is crucial for the Developer to not bore people with details to the point where people don't even want to pursue the dream anymore.

Some Developers let the details become negatives which scare people away from making the dream a reality. The punch-list gets to be so long that people start to evaluate whether it is even worth the time, effort, energy and allocation of resources to pursue the dream. Developers must walk the cliff's-edge of sharing enough details but not driving people to jump.

3) Never finishing the to-do list. There is a place for everyone on the team, to be sure. The Developer is mission-critical to the team and the process, but there comes a point when the Developer must hand off the details to others to make those things happen.

And yet, a true Developer keeps seeing details. And seeing details. And seeing details. So, it is possible for them to keep picking back up the list of details and adding more or refining. The danger here is that this can create frustrations.

When the checklist changes, the timeline changes. What people thought they were going to be able to accomplish by a particular deadline is now non-realistic due to changes in details.

When the check-list changes, the staffing can change. The number of people, or the type personnel required with the first list of details might shift significantly with a change to details.

And the more a Developer pursues the details, the more danger they run into of never finishing the list of details. This creates confusion and frustration. And it can actually hinder a project the Developer was trying to help make a success.

Blessed with the mind for details. Driven to do too much. This is the danger for the Developer which they must avoid. And it can be done. Here's how...

THE DEVELOPER'S DISCIPLINE

Like any of the other four leaders with a "D" on the team, the Developer must... interestingly enough... develop three strategic disciplines to help them stay on track and benefit the team. The team needs them to do this for there to be success. And those three disciplines are:

1) Enjoy the details privately, or with other Developers. As a leader with the Developer "D," you may be the only individual on the team with that role, or you may work with a team of Developers. (For example, many companies have entire departments of people devoted simply to development.) Whatever the case, learn the discipline of enjoying the details privately.

If you geek out on spreadsheets, graphs, charts, calendars, purchase orders, and task lists, that's awesome! Since everyone does not, keep something to write notes on with you and put all those thoughts, questions, and calculations down on. If you work by yourself as the primary Developer on the team, slip into your office or cubicle or closet or restroom and do a happy dance as you think about all the dreams you will make come true with the details you bring to the team.

If you work with a team of Developers, schedule a lunch together right after a vision-casting meeting and celebrate all the timelines and punch-lists you will have the opportunity to provide to help others do their job with excellence.

Scheme together... share ideas... point out why the other person's way won't work or is a stroke of genius which will save tons of money for the team.

The point is... Enjoy what you're gifted for with others who are gifted similarly. You'll both be glad you did. And those who can't appreciate it as much will not be burdened by something they don't really understand.

2) Share the process succinctly with the Dreamer. Give them only the broadest, big-picture look at the process--- to be shared with the team by the Dreamer, unless asked to share it yourself... then share it succinctly with the team. Details can be fleshed out later.

The Dreamer wants to know that the dream can indeed become reality and that someone can show them how to accomplish it. If they knew how to do it, they wouldn't need a Developer. But they don't know how, and that is why they are bringing you to the table. They need your expertise.

But the Dreamer cannot handle the full onslaught of details or they will get overwhelmed. You may try to utilize a lot of facts to prove the dream can become reality, but you may instead create a lot of roadblocks to it ever being accomplished.

Dreamers and Designers have very little heart for the mundane details it takes to make an exciting vision come about. They need minimized, generalized reports which give them a 30,000-foot overview. What is the cost analysis in a one-page report? How many people will this require? Do we have the equipment we need?

Give simple answers to those leaders unless they ask for more. If they ask for more, only expand a little bit. You can always give them more, but they can't always handle more all at once.

3) Break things into bite-sized chunks. Then break the chunks into bite-sized chunks so that people can handle the process. I suppose I could use the trite analogy given to tackling big projects of eating an elephant one bite at a time, and that would be okay. But I prefer to go at this with what the Israeli Defense Force uses as a model for what they do.

A couple years back, I was in Israel with a group of leaders and one of the folks speaking to us used to be in the IDF. They told us that the IDF uses a model whereby they break everything they do into three parts to simplify it. It doesn't matter whether it is a simple, everyday task or a major military offensive. They use the same model. Break everything into three parts. If each part is still too large, then break each of those parts into three parts. All any person needs to know at their level on the team is, "What are the three parts I'm responsible for helping accomplish?"

If you're a Developer, this would be a great tool to help you group details into chunks people can understand and accept. Not everyone needs every detail, and so leaders can determine who gets assigned which tasks. From there, more details can be added to break down those chunks further. This helps with both communication and keeping leaders from being overwhelmed. Like peeling back the layers of an onion, you can work through the details and help the team achieve its goal.

Developers... They bring functionality to the team. Developers show that the dream can work. They can inspire others to take this from the vision phase to the production phase. They are quite literally a hinge-pin determining whether or not the dream will ever get off the ground and become reality. They show the team what it will cost, how long it will take, what kind of manpower will be needed and what kind of work will have to be done for the goal to be accomplished. They are mission-critical.

Look at you and the team you're building! Country folk have a saying I often like to use.... "Now you're cookin' with gas." I may not be a chef, but I do know the interpretation of that colloquialism is that you are starting to do something the right way and will soon accomplish your goal. As a leader who is building a team, you now have a dream of something becoming greater than it is currently. That dream has been improved upon for greater potential. Plus, you actually have a plan for how that dream can become reality.

See, I told you anyone can lead. You just need the right team around you. And while your team is certainly beginning to take shape, there are still two more leaders you will need if you are going to reach your maximum potential.

CHAPTER 5

DELEGATORS

YOU KNOW WHO WE NEED TO HELP US, DON'T YOU?

IT'S PROBABLY NOT true, but it feels like my father-in-law has every tool known to mankind. Regardless of the task I come up against, he's always like, "Oh, hang on, I've got just the right (fill in the blank with the name of the appropriate tool for the occasion) you need to do that. What size do you need?" (You know, because he has every size I could possibly need.)

I, on the other hand, was not raised around too many tools. I think Mom had one of those "Her Tool Box" sets with a hammer, two screwdrivers (one flat head and one phillips head), a pair of pliers, a crescent wrench and a measuring tape. If we couldn't fix it with those tools in about 5 minutes, it was determined that we needed to call a repairman... or a friend who had more tools than us and actually knew what they were called.

For the record, I only know what some of those tools in "Her Tool Box" are called because I have learned about tools since I've been married. When I first came into "the family," I was, for all practical purposes, tool-less and lacking a significant amount of knowledge about how to use tools to build or fix anything.

Don't get me wrong. My parents gave me a lot of other tools in life... language tools, interpersonal tools, leadership tools, Scriptural tools... for which I am incredibly grateful, and with which I have tried to build great skills to serve God and others in life. I just did not have a toolbox of mechanical tools... like every man needs.

So it should come as no surprise to anyone that my first Christmas spent with Angela's family every gift I received was tools. And I was excited about it! I didn't know what some of them were called or how I would ever use them, but hey, I now had tools. I obviously assumed this made me more manly. So, we celebrated my new "ability" to build and repair things.

Over the years, I've amassed a small, but decent arsenal of tools... yes, the mechanical kind. I wouldn't say that I have all the tools I need for every job. In fact, many guys might look at my collection of tools and laugh. Truth be told, there might even be some women who would look at my collection of tools and laugh. But, in the last several years, I have found myself feeling more confident that I can fix something with the tools I have and without having to call someone else to repair it.

Now, I'll be straightforward... I do sometimes have to YouTube how to repair something. And I am not ashamed to call my father-in-law for help in knowing about building a project or fixing something that is broken. Since they live relatively close to us, he will sometimes offer to drive down and help me with the task. I almost always oblige. I wouldn't want to hurt his feelings, now would I?

When Daddy comes to help, he always brings the tools he thinks we will need, and some more that would make sense that we might need, to get the job done. We will be in the middle of a job, and I'll mention that we need a tool I'm not sure I have and he replies that he brought one with him. We go to the tool box in the back of his truck, and sure enough, there is the tool we need to complete the project. Somehow, it seems to make the task so much easier.

Whenever we complete a task, I try to always thank him and let him know how much I appreciate his help. Most of the times, it was more like me helping him. I tell him that I didn't realize it was that easy, and his standard reply, after deflecting any special ability on his part is, "Having the right tool makes all the difference in the world."

———

Now, a Dreamer can bring the vision of a better future to the table... and a Designer can enhance that dream with ideas and clarity for improved excellence... and a Developer can lay out a systematic plan which details exactly what it will take and how long it will take to make that dream become reality... but a Delegator brings the right tools to the project.

Please don't misunderstand. A company can have the right equipment. An organization may have the right supplies. It's just that when we think about the resources which will be required to complete a project or make a dream become reality, we often fail to underestimate human resources.

In an age when you drive through an automated car wash, make deposits as well as withdrawals from an ATM, self checkout at the store, and pay people from your smartphone, we can sometimes tend to think that we don't have to worry too much about the people in our "toolbox," but as my father-in-law so often reminds me, having the right tool to do the job makes it so much easier.

This is precisely why we all need a Delegator at the leadership table. They bring their expansive "toolbox" (aka, contact list) to any project, knowing just the right people needed to make the tasks happen in an excellent and timely manner. These people always "have a friend who makes this"... or a co-worker "who is incredible at that." They see a list of tasks which need to be accomplished, and pictures of people's faces who would be perfect for each of those tasks begin to scroll through their mind's eye.

So, while it is incredibly important to know what the dream is, how it can be made better, and what it is going to take to make it all happen, there is no replacing having the ability to pull together the actual people who will do the work of completing the project. It's Delegators who do that. They resource the team with people... the right people, for the right tasks.

The Delegators in leadership are like the general contractor who knows a framer... and an electrician... and a plumber... and a flooring specialist... and a drywall guy... and... and... and. Even on those rare occasions when they don't know just the right person, they know someone who knows just the right person.

It is the gifting of the Delegator to not only know people, but have the ability to sell them on the value of the project... to convince them that they want to be a part of this... to bring them onto the team. So, while we may not always realize it initially, we need Delegators more than we imagine.

This chapter is dedicated to helping each of us understand better what makes the Delegators tick, what can trip them up, and how they can best succeed. If you are a Delegator, this chapter is going to resonate with you. If you are not a Delegator, you are going to learn why you need them at the table with you.

So, let's get to it...

THE DELEGATOR'S DELIGHT

My friend, Jim, has more contacts on the contacts list on his phone than most people actually even know. To be accurate, at the time of writing this book, the exact number of people on Jim's contact list is 2,968 His friends on Facebook number more than 4,000.

Why does Jim have so many contacts? Simple, it's because Jim has so many friends. And whenever someone who knows Jim needs to get ahold of someone else whose contact info they do not have, they just ask Jim. Whenever someone needs someone to help them with something, but they don't believe they have the relational capital to get that person to help them, they ask Jim. Jim is a connector of friends. Jim knows people, and people know Jim. People love Jim. They want to help him. So, if he asks, they commit.

This is the delight of the Delegator. Their eyes light up when they realize that their network of relationships can be leveraged (in the most positive way) and brought into play to see the dream become reality. They find fulfillment and joy in the knowledge that they can pull together the team of workers who will actually be able to make things happen.

Delegators know people, and genuinely like people. They make friends and have friends. Some are closer than others, but they know people... a lot of people. True Delegators are not just "schmoozers" building a network of business contacts. They are building a base of friendships for a lifetime. They don't "make friends" so that they will have someone to look to later on in life on some particular job. They don't "wine and dine" people to get what they want. Delegators form and build genuine relationships, and down the road the people with whom they have become friends are happy to help when asked because they know the person doing the asking.

So when the leader of a project lays out the dream, shares the ideas that can make it better, then reveals the task list and timeline to get the job done, the Delegator immediately shifts into their world of relationships, building a list of team players who could best accomplish the work. This is where the Delegator shines. They can put together in their mind the right people for the right tasks.

Delegators use their "D" in leadership to process personalities, skill sets, level of availability, talent and fit within the team in order to bring the right people to the table for the accomplishment of the vision. They love sending the texts and emails or making the phone calls to engage people in joining the team. They will take someone to lunch and pitch the vision to get that person's buy-in.

Delegators make great human resource leaders. They have a knack for reading people and seeing where they best fit within the organization. They are terrific recruiters because they just get "the who's" who are gifted to tackle "the what's" in the fulfillment of a dream.

These team members are invaluable. You can have a powerful vision, terrific ideas, a masterful timeline and a meticulous task list, but if you don't have the right people who can do all that, all you have is wishful thinking.

The Delegator's delight is the people involved in the project. Let them focus on that, and they will find joy in their work.

THE DELEGATOR'S DILEMMA

The very delight of the Delegator can also be their dilemma. Sometimes Delegators are undervalued and/or misunderstood because they are not task-oriented. In a world of schedules, timelines and stats, Delegators can be championed initially, but can also be chastised later when they are viewed as those who seem less interested in the numbers and more in the process.

The truth is, people are messy and relationships take time. Willing wade into the swamp of what it takes to build relationships, Delegators can sometimes be labeled as not caring about the results.

While nothing may be further from the truth when it comes to results, what makes them tick is far different from that of the Dreamer or the Designer. They truly care about seeing the dream become reality, and their desire to help by building the team with the right players is evidence of that.

However, it can sometimes take time to convince someone that they should be a part of the team. It can take time to find the right person, who also happens to be available to jump on-board.

If you are both a Delegator and the assigned leader of a project or an assignment or a department, you can find yourself challenged by caring more about getting and keeping the right people on the team instead the overall accomplishment of your responsibility. As the primary leader, a Delegator must make sure they bring to the table the people who can fill in the blanks they leave in "getting it all done."

In a sense, the Delegator is trapped. They must be all about people to live in their sweet spot and bring its value to the table, but the flip side of that coin is that the very thing they bring to the table is what can most challenge their success.

THE DELEGATOR'S DANGER

The danger for the Delegator, then, is two-fold:

1) Being too carefree. Because their area of work expertise is people and they know it takes time to form relationships, the Delegator can become too carefree. They can have a thought process which tells them the timeline doesn't apply to them. They can begin to think that they are immune to schedule or calendar.

This is dangerous because people are counting on them. People can only wait so long to accomplish a task or complete a project. And if momentum slows to a crawl, or worse stops, then the dream everyone was pressing toward can end up dead in the water. This is especially bad if you, the Delegator, are also the primary leader.

2) Connecting and then checking out of the process. The truth is, we are almost all employees or team members. And while we each have a role to play and something to contribute, we must not think that our part is the only part we are ever required to play.

I suppose this could be included as a danger for each leadership "D," but this one seems to stand out to me as particularly important to address. For the Delegator, connecting the right people to the right assignments seem to be something that is a one-and-done type of role. In other words, it is easy for the

Delegator to fall into the faulty thinking that all they need to do is share the right names from their contact list, make a few introductions and then sit back and relax the rest of the project because "their work here is done."

If Delegators are not careful, they can make the connections between the leader and the right team players and then check out of the entire rest of the process. It can look like this...

"Bob, meet Jill. Jill is an amazing graphic designer and brand manager. She's exactly what we're looking for."

"Jill, meet Bob. Bob is the creative, driving force behind this dream we are working on. You will love what is going on here, and you will fit right in."

"Ok, great! See y'all at the finish line when we celebrate!"

That's when people start wondering what your role on the team really is. That's when people wonder why you're on the team. That's when people wonder if your paycheck is worth the investment. Just because you bring something to the team which is important does not give you the privilege to be lazy or check out.

People are counting on you to stay engaged in case they need someone else on the team. They are counting on you to be an ongoing contributor. In fact, sometimes a team member doesn't end up panning out like we thought they would and the leader will need to find someone else. How do they do that if you've checked out of the process?

THE DELEGATOR'S DISCIPLINE

What's a Delegator to do? How does one leverage their contact list effectively for the ultimate good of the team and the success of the vision? Here's how...

1) Be generous. Share who you know. You're the one with the connections. You're the one with the friends. You're the one with the massive contact list (or rolodex if you're really old school and have not digitized your life yet).

Don't be stingy. Sharing your relationships is what your team needs. Success will hinge on having the right people on-board. Some people bring what they know to the team... You bring who you know to the team. You can't live afraid that someone else is going to get your contact and not need you anymore. Keep building that contact list, and keep sharing.

2) Be timely. While everyone realizes that relationships take time, and connective communication doesn't always happen as quickly as we would like, the team still needs people when they need them.

Ask the team leader when they need to know who can fill each role. Ask them how much time, effort and energy they would like for you to spend in pursuing hard-to-get people for the project.

If you are still striking out at filling a particular role, ask if they would prefer for you to move on to look for someone else. Let them know how long changing horses midstream would take, but always work within your allotted time frame.

3) Be responsible. Stay engaged with both your leader and the people you recommend for various roles. Ask how things are going.

Take some initiative. Do some follow-up. See if there are any other folks which you might need to bring to the table. Ask if there is anything else you can do to help bring a better connection between the people you recommend and the rest of the team. You already have relationship on both sides and can help navigate relational issues which might arise.

In 1985, one of my favorite TV series was "Stingray". Ray, the main character of the show, who drove a classic Stingray Corvette was a man of mystery who would come to the aid of people in need. (Think of a mix between private detective, former special forces, spy and pool shark.). Those in need would find out about him in the newspaper classified section and contact him for help. Ray would show up mysteriously soon after, listen to their problem and decide whether or not he would "take their case." (He always took the case... otherwise there wouldn't have been a show.)

The cool twist of the show, which could not be truly appreciated until you had watched several episodes, was the manner of payment. The people hiring Stingray were always desperate enough to pay whatever he asked. No fee was too high.

His response was always startling to them. He would say something like, "I won't accept payment in money, but one day I will need something you can provide. When I come to you and ask you for it, you must do it. You will not be able to turn me down at that point." And in future episodes, you would see the people who Ray had helped previously show up once again as the solution to the problem encountered in the current show's need.

For all practical purposes, Stingray was the ultimate Delegator. He always knew just the right person to help in any given situation. He was always able to leverage his relationship with them to the benefit of someone else. And that someone else was at the same time becoming someone he would reach out to later for help.

Now all analogies eventually break down, and I understand that some would perceive my illustration of Stingray to be negative and manipulative. But the point is that Delegators build relationships over time which later become a resource which few can tap into as they can.

———∞———

Delegators bring the right people to the team. They show us that the dream can become reality if we bring the right people into the right roles. They inspire others to take the dream from the written page to those people who can actually make it happen. Delegators are quite literally a hinge-pin between a really well-designed dream-plan and getting the wheels of production into motion. They show the team how finding the right players can give the whole team a victory. They are mission-critical.

At this point, you may be looking at the team you've built and be tempted to think you have everyone you need, but it would be a mistake to stop this close to the finish line. Those people the Delegator leader told you about? They're the last piece of the puzzle. Build on!

CHAPTER 6

DOERS

YOU KNOW HOW LONG THE TO-DO LIST IS, DON'T YOU?

I USED TO lead summer camps and a winter camp each year for the students of our denomination in our state. Over the time I served in that role, we led 44 camps in all. I don't know if you've ever been to a camp for teenagers, but I can tell you from a lot of experience that it takes *A LOT* of people tackling *A LOT* of tasks to make everything work.

For each camp, we typically invited 30-60 volunteer staff to help us make things happen. Most were high school and college-aged students, but some were adults all the way up into their 60's. These wonderful folks set up the stage in the auditorium, stocked bathrooms in dorms with paper goods, cleaned dishes, collected trash, ran games, worked the concession stand, cooked meals, swept, mopped, vacuumed, and a whole plethora of other tasks as needs arose. By the end of a camp, they had enjoyed great times working together and were flat-out tired.

Some of our best volunteers were those who really enjoyed working a task list. They were the kind who would show up earlier than expected and ask where the list of things was which needed to be accomplished. The more lengthy the list, the more they engaged to make it all happen.

Those who were gluttons for punishment- and the fun we all had along the way together- would return camp after camp to serve with us. They began earning titles like veteran and ultra-veteran the longer they served. I vividly remember two young ladies who served with us for several years who were nicknamed "the robots"— they had incredible attitudes, provided no drama, and simply cranked out work like they were... well... robots. And they became the gold standard for those who wanted to serve with us at camps.

This was great for me because I had a vision in my mind of what that week of camp would be like. Angela would come along and give me ways to make it even better. Others on our leadership team helped me create timelines and budgets and task lists, and usually someone helped me recruit these volunteers.

But there always came that moment on the first day the staff would arrive... usually a couple days before the campers and sponsors arrived for the camp to start... when I would look at the long list of tasks which had to be accomplished in order for everything to work, and I would feel a bit overwhelmed. That's when these kind folks who got very little- like a t-shirt and some free food and a little gas money- in return for their services would arrive and take the bull by the horns.

Suddenly, the choking feeling of "it's never going to get done" would loosen its grip on me, and I could begin to see that the dream really would become a reality. My appreciation for those leaders with the "Doer" leadership "D" soared. I could not have been more grateful. I understood very clearly that without the Doers, our dreams and plans were nothing more than a wish and a prayer.

There is not an organization, business, church or even a family which could survive a week without Doers. Doers make it happen. Others dream and scheme and plan and build teams, but doers get the job across the finish line.

NOTE: Let pause here to de-bunk a common misconception regarding leadership, teams and Doers. Many leaders sadly and incorrectly believe that all they really need to have is a group of Doers to take their project or assignment to completion.

I led that way for awhile. I had the dream and just needed some hands and feet to get it done, but it was never that simple. I ended up discovering that we needed the other leadership "D's" at the table as well in order for everything to come together as best as it possibly could.

So, while this chapter will delight those who lead and want to make sure it all gets done, be sure not to misconstrue or misunderstand the total value of those with the Doer leadership "D." One of the best leaders to ever serve on one of our teams— and actually took on an assignment from us which involved tackling an entire major area of leadership— was a Doer.

Doers are not just grunts. They are not just unskilled labor. Benjamin Franklin said, "Motivation is when your dreams put work clothes on."[3] Doers can lead. And this chapter focuses on what it means for a Doer to use their "D" in leadership to make an impact for their organization.

With that in mind, let's get at it...

THE DOER'S DELIGHT

A couple of my favorite paraphrased quotes from Doers who have led with us are...

> *"I'm perfectly content to just check off the to-do list you give me, and you can handle the stress of all that other stuff."*

> *"Why don't you just go shake hands and kiss babies or whatever it is that you do and let us take care of all this stuff."*

It was funny when they said those things, but the great thing is that they meant those words. They knew their strength and joy in leading.

That is because the leader with the Doer "D" delights in the task list. They want to "get it done." Every time a check mark or strikethrough marks another task accomplished, they feel something light up on the inside of themselves. Accomplishment provides fulfillment for the Doer.

Hand a Doer a task list on a clipboard or add them to a work-group on a to-do app, and they are happier than a hog in the mud on a sunny day. For the Doer, they delight in knowing what has to be done and the time by when it needs to be completed.

The joy is in the knowing. It is in the clarity. It is in the simplicity of it all. The Doer enjoys straightforward conversation and work...

> *"Would you please do these tasks for us?"*
> *"I need these twelve items accomplished by this Friday."*
> *"Please paint this sign's background red and the lettering white."*

No wondering. No guessing. No frills. Just a direct request and fulfillment of that request.

They have a sense of having done what was needed when a task is accomplished. They have a sense that, with their own two hands, they have done something to move the project forward or to make the dream become a reality.

In a sense, the Doer is closest to the reality stage. They are some of the first to see the fulfillment of what was once just a dream in someone's head and heart. It is like they get an early glimpse into what others will soon enjoy.

And they also get the early joy of knowing that, without them doing their part, others would not get to experience what is being produced. It really is about producing for them.

Sure everyone on the team has to deliver or produce in some way. But nowhere is it more clear than with the Doer. And in no one else is there that same contentment in the heart as is in the Doer's when they have checked the final item off their list as being completed.

THE DOER'S DILEMMA

The greatest dilemma for a Doer is being misunderstood. Because of their bent toward getting it all done, Doers can be misunderstood in two different ways:

1) They become viewed as grunts of the team. People can tend to view Doers as not being great leaders because they just want to tackle a to-do list.

I once served on a team of excellent leaders who were all incredibly capable of leading well. And yet one player on the team always got the "low-man-on-the-totem-pole" jobs because he loved serving and tackling a massive to-do list. He is a get-it-done guy and so those were the jobs which were assigned to him.

Now this man is an amazing leader who leads teams of leaders himself. He is very educated and talented in a wide variety of areas. I have had opportunities to hear him teach leadership and had him share his leadership strategies with me one-on-one. His leadership abilities would blow you away.

And yet he was always assigned the simplest, most routine tasks of anyone on our team, because he has the Doer leadership "D."

It can be a difficult thing for a Doer to overcome the mentality that they can only do the simplest, most menial tasks in the organization. In fact, it takes a great deal of effort on their part- and on the part of the rest of the team- to not view them in this light.

2) People assume they are terrific, all-around leaders. This is perhaps less obvious, but it is the exact opposite of the first shade of the Doer's dilemma. People see them as "go-getters" or "get-the-job-done-folks" and think they are capable of anything as leaders. And they are great leaders... in their own element.

But what some "higher-ups" do is inaccurately define the Doer and try to put them in a role which requires them to lead from a position which they were not designed for. They are not Dreamers or Designers who are going to have great vision or enhancing ideas. They are not Developers who can lay out a detailed plan for how things must work to achieve the desired outcome. And they are not even Delegators with a network of people who are just right for any task.

Yet, because of their abilities in getting assignments across the finish line, they are labeled as leaders who can do anything. That's just it... They can DO anything. But they may not be able to dream anything... or design it... or develop it... or delegate it.

And so the Doer can sometimes be placed in a role of leadership for which they were not designed. And some Doers can feel so thrown off by what is now being asked of them, that they freeze up and in so doing disappoint those who thought they could do anything.

THE DOER'S DANGER

The danger, then, for the Doer is allowing those two shades of their dilemma to cause them to behave in one of two ways which are both equally as harmful to their leadership.

The first behavior which is dangerous for a Doer is in allowing themselves to become so task-oriented that they don't develop their people skills adequately. Because their delight is in completing the task list, interacting with people can seem like a waste of time... a distraction from "what is really important."

Having served in a variety of ministry roles over the past twenty years, it is always funny to me to hear some other minister comment about how much easier and more enjoyable ministry would be if it were not for all the people with whom they have to deal. "People-less ministry." That, my friends, is an oxymoron. If there were no people, then there would be no one needing ministry. I get what they usually mean. They are just implying that it is the fact people are involved which makes things messy and challenging. Most of them truly love people and understand that ministry is about helping and serving people.

However, I have known a few Doers over the years who truly would prefer to not have to deal with other people. Stick them at a computer entering data... or at a sink washing dishes... or on a truck hauling freight... and they are content.

The problem here is that, unless you are going to become a self-sufficient hermit living removed from all society on the backside of some remote wilderness, you are eventually going to have to deal with people. And as a leader, to be successful at anything, you are going to have to have at least a bare-minimum level of healthy people skills.

I'm not inferring that you have to be like Will Rogers, who never met a man he didn't like. I'm simply suggesting that it is a danger for the Doer to think that they can function successfully in any kind of organization (business, church or even family) by avoiding people and simply doing tasks. If they are not careful, because they don't want to be asked to lead or deal with people, they just stick their nose in a task list and mind their own business.

The second behavior which is dangerous for a Doer is in allowing themselves to become mentally lazy. This can stem from others viewing them as part of the grunt labor caste. Left unchecked, this mentality can seep into their own thinking and they can begin to view themselves as simply a person who completes to-do lists.

This self-image is dangerous because it devalues who the Doer really is as a person and as a leader. It causes people to think that workers like them are a-dime-a-dozen. And when others treat them that way, they can be tempted to reduce what they believe they are capable of doing. When they believe they are a-dime-a-dozen, they lose heart in what they are doing and figure they can do menial tasks anywhere, for anyone.

Doers can be great leaders, but this danger is one that can trip them up ever so easily. When they view themselves as less than significant leaders on the team, they can let their mental acuity begin to slip. They don't feel like they need to learn anything new... or try anything new... or stretch themselves. And in doing so, they give others reason to believe that they are not motivated or progressing.

I'm certainly not suggesting that every person has to pursue continual formal education. Not everyone desires that or functions well in those settings. However, in today's world with access to so many ways to learn so much, we as leaders should never have any reason for not continuing to develop ourselves in some way. Doers could refine their skill set to accomplish more or accomplish what they do more simply. Doers could learn how to do other tasks within the same field and expand their ability to serve.

What Doers cannot afford to do is fall into the dangerous traps of not developing their people skills and/or becoming mentally lazy.

THE DOER'S DISCIPLINE

In order for a leader with the Doer leadership "D" to avoid these dangers and be the tremendous leader they are, they must apply the following discipline to their lives:

1) Stay engaged with the team. As a team member, the primary discipline of the Doer leader is to stay engaged with others on the team in such a way that they understand others and others understand them. Because they can be so easily misunderstood, sometimes a Doer must work a little extra at connecting with people. That can come in the form of asking questions about the dream which they are helping become a reality, or by casually letting others know about new skills or knowledge you are acquiring. Every small effort put forth to show people that you care about more than tasks and that you are more than a grunt will help secure your value to the team.

2) Do what you do... with a twist. If you happen to be one of those Doers who earned a leadership role/title because you just kept getting things done and now you find yourself not "doing" anymore, you have a unique discipline. Your supervisors probably expect you to apply that same "doing" to dreaming, planning, strategizing, etc., not realizing at all that they took you out of your element. That's okay.

Do exactly that. View your role as "doing" and begin by making yourself a task list which involves gathering the right team members around you who can dream, design, develop and delegate. Invite them to do what they do and to let you do what you do.

Let them dream, scheme, lay out processes and invite others to help. And ask them for a task list a mile long along the way. Then you do what you... well... do. Your supervisors will still view you as getting the job done, and you will still get to do what you enjoy... doing.

———

We need Doers because they get stuff done. Doers show us that the dream can become reality when we apply a little elbow grease. They are the ones who make the rest of us shine. Doers make sure everything is accomplished, and then they hand the clipboard back to us as if to ask, "Is that all you've got?" They are impressive in their own right. Without Doers, all the dreams and plans simply lay on a shelf, collect dust and leave us feeling empty about what might have been.

I raise my mug of strong, black coffee to all the Doers in this world. On more than one occasion, I wish had more of what you have... that innate ability to blow through a list of tasks in no time flat and make it look so easy. I simply sit back in amazement when you build... and clean... and stack... and haul... and label... and organize... and enter data... and measure... and... and... and. It seems like you can accomplish anything anyone can dream up.

So here's to you... all the veterans, ultra-veterans and robots! Keep doing that thing you do!

You now have an understanding of the key players you need on your team. The challenge going forward with this new knowledge is where most leadership books leave us wanting more. What you most need now is the steps necessary to implement this concept. It's not difficult. In fact, it's quite simple:

1) *Discover your own leadership "D" and help those potential team members around you discover theirs.*
2) *Learn how to find, attract, and invite the right team members whom you need to help you accomplish your assignments.*

To help you accomplish this, in the next section, I have designed a quiz to help you discover which "D" you have received in leadership. Then, in the chapter after that, we will look at exactly how to find, attract, and invite those team members with the other four leadership "D's."

Let me encourage you one more time before we move on. Whether you believe it or not, you are a phenomenal leader. You have ability, skill and talent that every team needs. You can improve your own leadership, as well as help others improve theirs. You are going to build a great team and accomplish more than ever before. Seize the "D!"

BRINGING THEM TO THE TABLE

CHAPTER 7

TAKE THE QUIZ - FIND YOUR SUPERPOWER

NOW THAT YOU know about each leadership "D," it's time to hone down which ones you might have received. I say that in the plural because most people have one primary leadership "D" and then one which is close but secondary. This provides for the overlap and hand-off necessary for great team fluidity and function.

This is a personalized quiz... not a test. There are no right or wrong answers. Everyone has abilities to bring to the table. Anyone can be a great leader when they realize the leadership "D" which they have received and apply these principles with their team.

Please check only one statement from each section. The key to this quiz giving you the clearest result is to check only the statements which you really feel strongly represent you and connect with you. When in doubt, choose the statement which most closely represents your thoughts, feelings or attitudes.

If you prefer, you may take the quiz online for free at allenchapin.com by clicking on the "Leadership 'D' Quiz" tab in the top menu, and the online version will score the quiz for you. Additionally, feel free to share the quiz online via social media or email to see which leadership "D's" your co-workers and friends have. Then as you begin to find out which leadership "D" those around you have, you will be ready to invite them to join your team in order to accomplish what once seemed difficult or impossible.

For now, with no further ado, let's discover your leadership "D"...

TIMELINES...

_____1. irritate me.

_____2. are irrelevant to me.

_____3. are for other people to deal with.

_____4. excite me.

_____5. motivate me.

PEOPLE ARE OFTEN AMAZED AT...

_____6. how much I can accomplish.

_____7. how easily I see how pieces of a process fit together.

_____8. the creative ideas I have to improve something.

_____9. the number of contacts I have on my phone.

_____10. my ability to see a brighter future.

I AM MOST ENERGIZED BY...

_____11. having business lunches.

_____12. having a sandwich while I lay out plans.

_____13. having coffee by myself with time to think.

_____14. having heard an idea which makes me forget to eat because I am too busy researching how to take it to the next level.

_____15. having a meal to celebrate what I have completed.

SOCIAL MEDIA IS...

_____16. for finding ideas about how something could be improved upon or done differently.

_____17. exclusively for staying connected with people.

_____18. for those people who are not as busy as I am getting things done.

_____19. simply computer algorithms which I could figure out if I had the time and tools.

_____20. always evolving, and I can imagine what the next social media hit should be.

PEOPLE SOMETIMES MISUNDERSTAND MY...

_____21. suggestions as correcting them.

_____22. ideas as living in a fantasy world.

_____23. desire to get the job finished as not being interested in people's feelings.

_____24. attention to details as perfectionism.

_____25. time spent hanging out with others as goofing off.

STATISTICS...
_____26. take time away from me accomplishing something important.

_____27. show me how processes could be streamlined.

_____28. make me think of people I know who fit into certain categories.

_____29. could be presented more effectively so that people could understand and use them.

_____30. reveal future trends which point us in the right direction.

I LOVE...
_____31. planning and scheduling.

_____32. having time to myself to think about the future.

_____33. tweaking things to make them better.

_____34. making new friends.

_____35. working with my hands.

I ENJOY...
_____36. new ideas.

_____37. how-to manuals.

_____38. researching ways to do one thing well.

_____39. lists.

_____40. introducing people to others who can help them.

I THINK IN TERMS OF...

_____41. meetings, phone calls and texts needed to accomplish something.

_____42. how much is left in order to accomplish something.

_____43. budgets, supplies and personnel needed to accomplish something.

_____44. finding things that others miss.

_____45. potential and possibilities.

I PREFER...

_____46. tasks.

_____47. people.

_____48. processes.

_____49. dreams.

_____50. excellence.

Leadership "D" Identification Guide

Awesome! You completed the quiz. You are one step closer to becoming a more effective leader. Now let's see which leadership "D" designation most reflects you.

On each line below, write the number of statements from the list under that line which you checked. The leadership "D" designation with the highest number is most likely the "D" you have been given. And while it is not scientifically foolproof, it is a great place to begin as you discover your leadership giftedness and build your team.

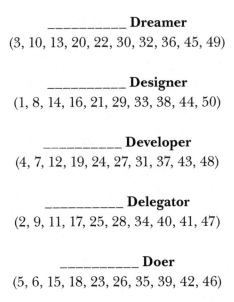

_____ **Dreamer**
(3, 10, 13, 20, 22, 30, 32, 36, 45, 49)

_____ **Designer**
(1, 8, 14, 16, 21, 29, 33, 38, 44, 50)

_____ **Developer**
(4, 7, 12, 19, 24, 27, 31, 37, 43, 48)

_____ **Delegator**
(2, 9, 11, 17, 25, 28, 34, 40, 41, 47)

_____ **Doer**
(5, 6, 15, 18, 23, 26, 35, 39, 42, 46)

So, which leadership "D" did you score the highest in? That is most likely your primary leadership "D" designation. And the next closest score is most likely your secondary leadership "D" designation. Typically, they will be two that are close to each other, though not always. Each individual has God-given abilities which are unique to them.

Were you almost evenly balanced across the board? Fantastic! You will be able to relate to a lot of other leaders in their "D" strengths, but go ahead and focus on that highest number category first and foremost. It is still most likely your greatest leadership "D."

Now that you know your leadership "D" designation, this knowledge will help you better serve any team you find yourself on. If you are not the primary leader on your team, knowing your leadership "D" will help you be able to communicate with the primary leader how you feel you will best be able to serve them.

Of course, I am making an assumption that because you are reading this book, you are a primary leader in at least some role in your life. With that in mind, in the next chapter we will focus on how to find, attract, and invite the other four leadership "D" leaders to the table with you so that you can have a complete, functional team and achieve the greatest success.

CHAPTER 8

FIND, ATTRACT AND INVITE THE RIGHT "D'S"

THE GREAT BASKETBALL coach, Phil Jackson, said, "The strength of the team is each individual member. The strength of each member is the team."[4] That is a pretty big statement from the man who coached the player who might be the greatest basketball player of all times. Yet he sold his players on this "Phil-osophy" and as a result, they went on to be one of the greatest teams of all times. Additionally, each player became a better player individually because of the rest of their team.

I love that statement so much because it says that our individual gifts and talents are unique, important and special. They make us valuable to others on our team. But I also love it because it says that we each need others, and no one can do everything by themselves.

To believe only one or the other is true is to make a leadership error of astronomical proportions. To believe we cannot lead... to believe we have no talents or abilities of value... to believe we do not bring anything essential to the success of the team... well, that is self-demeaning, God-dishonoring and simply untrue. And to believe we have it all together... to believe we are so multi-talented that we need no one else... to believe can accomplish more without others getting in our way... well, that is arrogant, God-opposing, and simply untrue.

There is great benefit to finding the balance. There is health in leadership when we can honestly and confidently say, "I know I have received a leadership 'D' which can help our team, but I also know that I need other leadership 'D's' on this team in order to be the best we can possibly be."

This is the basis upon which great teams are built, and from which great accomplishments are achieved. This is when dreams become reality. This is when we can truly do something worthwhile to make a difference in this world.

Now, before we get into the practics of finding, attracting and inviting the right leadership "D's" to serve on our teams, we need to address a few questions you might have already starting to brew in the back of your mind.

For example, "What if I'm not the primary leader on the team?" Good question. I know I addressed it briefly at the end of the last chapter with the quiz, but let me go into greater detail.

All you can do is be the best leader you can possibly be. Knowing your area of strength and operating in that area is your best bet at being successful on the team.

When I was in my early twenties and just credentialed with our denomination, I expressed my frustration to my Dad, who was at that time a leader in our denomination in the area where we lived. He gave me this advice..

"Allen, you can only impact your area of influence. If you disagree with something, make the change or set the standard you believe is correct in the area where you have influence. Then be faithful there.

When people are looking for leaders to lead them, they choose people who have held to their convictions and made a difference in the area they lead. If the Lord is willing, then perhaps they will choose you to lead in the future, and your area of influence will expand. At that point, you can bring your ideas and changes to that broader area.

As time goes by, when people are looking for leaders to take on larger spheres of influence, they will look for people who have been successful at bringing about positive changes and still held strong to their convictions. If the Lord is willing, then perhaps they will choose you to lead in the future, and your area of influence will expand. At that point, you can bring your ideas and changes to that even broader area.

Eventually, you will either have the ear of those who have the greatest area of influence, or you will be asked to lead yourself. At that point, you can influence the broad area you'd like to see changed right now because you will have earned the trust of many people along the way."

That was good advice which has served me well over the years. In essence, Dad was trying to explain to me that I could only affect the area in which I had leadership at the time.

The same is true when you are on a team, but are not the primary leader. Simply focus on the area you can influence, share your thoughts with those who lead, and work hard to see the team succeed. In doing so, people who make the decisions will see your efforts and take note. Then they will either want to hear more of what you have to say, or perhaps they will give you an increased leadership role.

Another question you might ask is, "What do I do if I don't get to pick my own team? What if I inherit a team?"

Great question because this happens to people all the time. Teams are assigned by a leader and you are asked to lead a team made up of players whom you did not choose. And perhaps the overall leader didn't practice what I am proposing here. Perhaps they put five Dreamers and one Delegator on the team.

You probably cannot change the assignments. However, this may not mean that you cannot invite more people to the team. Or maybe you can even create some sub-teams to break the assignment down into bite-sized chunks. Since you are the primary leader of this area of influence, you can choose who those people will be, and you can choose to make sure teams are outfitted with all five leadership "D's."

If you do well with the assignment, your team will take notice, and so will your superiors. Then perhaps you will have the opportunity to share with them what you feel helped you succeed. That's when you share what you've learned here and sound like a leadership genius. But in all seriousness, it may be the open door to seeing this principle instituted in the future so that you will have made an impact on your organization and expanded your influence.

Last question before we move on to the practical outworking of building your team... "How do I avoid attracting the same "D's" when that is natural?" Excellent question! I like the way you think.

We all know like attracts like. We all like to have people like us around us. That's comfortable to us. If we're Dreamers, we enjoy being around other Dreamers because they "get us." Doers like having other Doers around because they feel like they can just get the job done and not have to fool with all that other stuff. It's just human nature to want to keep things comfortable. Like people are attracted to like people. It happens.

Much of my adult work life has been working in and through the Church. As such, I have had the opportunity to see numerous types and styles of churches and leaders. It's always been amazing to me how lead pastors who are musical attract tons of great musicians while other churches struggle to do so, regardless of location. I've also seen lead pastors with significant administrative skills attract all kinds of business leaders. It's because like attracts like.

To avoid this, we have to put forth considerably focused, intentional effort at building our teams. We all need people like us... people who "get us"... to hang out with. This doesn't mean they have to be on the team. They can be friends without being on the team. They can be a part of your support system without having an official role. If you feel like you will hurt someone's feelings whom you really like because they have the same leadership "D" as you, explain what you are doing in building your team and how you'd like them to come alongside you in a different role. Most people will understand, and you will have a great friend along with a terrific team.

And now to quote almost every TV or movie judge ever, "If there are no more questions..."

Let's put some feet to our theories here. Let's suppose that you are the leader of a team. And let's suppose that you are wondering how to find, attract and invite leaders with the other four leadership "D's" to join your team for maximum potential for success.

Under each of the following designations, I want to discuss how to find that leadership "D"... what you can do to make being on your team attractive to them so that they want to join it... and how to best go at officially inviting them to be a part of your team. Some of it will seem obvious, but hopefully it will give perspective on how to relate to them in order to build your best team.

One final note before we dive in... The secret to making your invitation to any one of these leaders is humility. You have to be willing to admit that you can't do it all by yourself... that you need help... that you lack something which someone else has... that you are not intimidated by the fact that you don't have it all together. If you act superior, or that you just want to include others so that you look like a better leader, you will fail miserably. All truly great leaders have been humble as well as gifted.

Fabled King Arthur understood this concept. It is said of him that he created a large round table where he would gather his greatest knights (aka, team members) to discuss matters of great importance. Legend tells that he made the table round so that every person at the table was considered of equal importance. All would remove their armor and accoutrements and sit as equals at the table. The knights viewed him no less as king because he did not posture himself that way. Instead, they valued him even more because he humbled himself and valued them.

So, let's take this moment to climb down off that high horse culture tries to make us all mount, and let's commit to be genuine, honest, sincere and humble as you approach others to invite them to help you succeed at greatness.

With all this foundation set in place, let's look at how to find, attract and invite leaders to join the team we lead and sit at our round table...

DREAMER

Every team needs at least one Dreamer. Usually, one is enough. More than one creates multiple visions and directions in which to go. It's not that any of those visions are wrong... just different. The team needs to stay focused on bringing one dream into reality.

If you are not a Dreamer leader, then this may seem like the most daunting team member to find, attract and invite. We typically assume that they are already leading their own team, and often they are due to the perceptions we have of that type person discussed in that section of this book.

The truth is that Dreamers love to dream. If given the opportunity, they will probably gladly add another opportunity to dream to their plate. It is almost as if they cannot help themselves. They practically salivate over the opportunity to look into a situation, evaluate it and perceive what it can become. So, don't assume they are unreachable or unattainable.

FIND DREAMERS:

Dreamers are visionary. So, look for them in places you would expect to find them. Look for the person standing at the window staring out, lost in thought. Look for the person who is always watching inspiring TED talks... or checking out the debut of the latest Apple product... or going to movies about people who made significant contributions in this world.

Additionally, look for those leaders who are not satisfied with how things are right now. While their distaste for the current condition of things can drive people nuts because they never seem to be satisfied with the status quo, that is a huge clue to you that they just might be a Dreamer. Or a spoiled brat. But let's go for Dreamer to begin with and believe the best in people.

ATTRACT DREAMERS:

Dreamers are visionary. The key to attracting them to your team is to sell them on the "why" behind this assignment. Show them how you feel their expertise would help you accomplish your own "dream," to succeed at your assignment and why it is such a big deal to you.

I have a friend who works for a leader whose mission in life is to impact the entire world... like the whole planet of people. This friend told me that he learned very quickly when he came into staff meetings to either bring an idea which would impact the entire world or else sit there quietly. He discovered that if his idea wasn't big enough in his leader's eyes, it would be dismissed or he would be challenged to expand it. But if he could show how the idea had the potential to impact the entire world, then it would always be funded almost instantly and without question.

If you want to attract a Dreamer to your team, you have to be able to show them how you feel their contribution is going to change things, make things better. They have to know there is room for them to cut loose with their dreaming and bring something before thought impossible to the table for consideration.

INVITE DREAMERS:

Dreamers are visionary. Let them know that you need to know what the possibilities are, that it's difficult for you to read future trends, etc.

Your invitation has to be an invitation to something bigger than you... bigger than them... bigger than anyone can imagine. Regardless of how simple or mundane the assignment is, you need to find a way for it to be more as you invite a Dreamer to the team. If you can't see it yourself, this is the perfect opportunity to express to them why you need them on your team. You can say something like, "I know this may seem like a pretty simple, straightforward project, but I believe there could be more to it and we could make a significant contribution to our organization if I just had someone on the team who could see what we are all missing."

As a fisherman, I like to fish with light tackle for bream and crappie. I like to fish with a pole and a cork. There is this sense of anticipation when you see the cork begin to bounce a little because you know a fish is starting to check it out... that they are tempted to inhale the bait. And then all of a sudden the cork goes under and they're hooked.

In the same way, when you invite a Dreamer to dream for the team and you invite them properly, you can see when they are hooked on the possibilities... and you've got yourself another great team member!

DESIGNER

Every team needs a great Designer. Actually, this is one of those team members where more than one might be helpful. So don't stress if you end up with more than one on your team. It might actually work out to the team's advantage.

You might think that Designers would be difficult to identify because they can be confused with Dreamers as a result of all their ideas, but their ideas often springboard from the vision put forth by a Dreamer.

Designers are generally in demand because of their creativity. It seems everyone wants them on their team. Don't let the fact that they are in high demand keep you from approaching them to be on your team. Your team needs them to be its best, and with the right approach you can land a Designer leader on your team. Then watch your team's effectiveness multiply.

FIND DESIGNERS:

Designers are creative. Listen for people who are on Pinterest all the time and showing someone what they just found. They're the ones always telling someone about another way or a better way to do something. They are the people asking someone with an idea who doesn't know how to accomplish it, "Well, have you Googled it? Hang on, let me look..."

Listen for the person who is always saying, "Oh, you know what you could do, don't you?" This is the one whose eyes light up and wheels start turning when they hear about the possibility for a different future, but they are not satisfied with the new future as presented. Find the people who are always full of ideas in meetings and the boss has to shut them down so that the meeting can progress.

These people may have magazines all over their desks at work or their coffee tables at home. It's because they are interested in ideas which make things better. They are the ones who are always telling someone, "Oh, I just saw something that would make this amazing!"

Like Dreamers, they live with a certain level of discontent with much in life. They think there must be a better mousetrap... a better drive-thru concept... a better whatever. There always has to be a better way than the way things are being done currently.

Find a person with an idea for a better way, and you have probably identified a Designer. And now you need to attract them to your team.

ATTRACT DESIGNERS:
Designers are creative. If you're not a Designer, then you definitely need them on your team. The key to getting them on board with your team is to sell them on the "what" of the assignment. It's best to attract them by expressing your objective, but let them know that you feel like there must be more to it... that there has to be a better way to do this than others normally do.

To attract Designer leaders, you need them to know that you are interested in taking this to the next level. Terms like "upgrade" or "level up" or "excellence" speak their native tongue.

The idea here is to let them see that you believe there is room for improvement on almost any idea or assignment. Let them know you understand that sometimes things need to go "over the top" and that sometimes "simpler is better." Regardless, no art can become a masterpiece until it has had those finishing touches added to it. This is what Designers bring to the team.

INVITE DESIGNERS:
Designers are creative. Let them know that you are lacking those extra touches... that creativity that really makes things zing... that you feel you don't have the ideas to take this up a notch.

Your invitation cannot be standard. I'm not saying you have to become ultra-creative. They just need a compelling enough invitation to be drawn in.

Your invite to them might be couched in phraseology like this... "Look, this could be great if I could just find someone who really knows how to add some flair, some pizazz to the norm and make it special. I've noticed that you seem to have a knack for seeing how to do things with a high level of creativity and excellence, and we're looking for someone who can bring that to this project.."

When they see that there is someone who is interested in hearing their creative ideas... and truly considering those ideas... they will leap at the opportunity to live in their leadership "D."

—∞—

DEVELOPER

Every team needs at least one Developer, but can utilize more than one depending on the breadth and scope of the project. Developers can be specifically chosen based on the need at hand. Or they can be chosen because they have an extremely broad base of knowledge and skills which will help produce the right timeline, process and budget.

It is possible to think that Developers are always busy and never have time to give to pull together all the details for another assignment, but they do it with such ease that it probably will not be too much of a struggle to get them to say "yes" to your invitation.

Sure everyone wants their expertise, but Developers are masters of balance... and planning... and scheduling. So, be encouraged. You can almost certainly uncover a Developer leader who will help you. And you need them to help you actually produce a plan which will produce a result.

FIND DEVELOPERS:

Developers are strategic. So when you are trying to find a leader with the Developer "D" for your team, look for those who get totally lost in the details. Look for those who are always explaining how things work. Try to find the "bean counters" or the "tech wizards."

Another way to find a Developer is to find that person who is always willing to teach someone else how to do something. They are patient in the process. They don't get frustrated in the grueling step-by-step process of helping someone else learn.

Who is it in your life or organization who really knows how to set a budget and stick to it? Who is it who is always thinking about the calendar and the clock? Who is it who is always checking to make sure you have all the supplies you need?

Find someone who fits these descriptions, and you are hot on the trail of locating a Developer.

ATTRACT DEVELOPERS:
Developers are strategic. The key to creating a desire in the Developer to be on the team is to sell them on the "how" of the assignment. I'm not saying to play dumb here, but the truth is that you may truly not know how to make a plan work. It doesn't hurt to let that part show to those who really do know how to make a plan work. It's attractive to them.

If you truly want to attract Developers to your team, then you have to create the opportunity for them to do what they do... strategize. You have to make room for them to plan, schedule, calculate, estimate and scheme. Let them know that you are looking for someone who has the capacity and ability to help develop process so that the rest of the team can do their parts to get the assignment or project completed.

INVITE DEVELOPERS:
Developers are strategic. The "pie in the sky" approach is not going to work with them. You can't bluff your way through this one. Mumbo-jumbo, catchphrases and lofty ideas are not going to help you here. As challenging as it might be for you,

you are going to have to craft your own strategic invitation. They are going to need to see that you believe in planning and scheduling.

Begin by doing a little research. Find out where or what they like to eat. Contact them to see if they are free on a particular day at a specific time of day for a set length of time. For example, it might be that you invite them to lunch at their favorite restaurant this Thursday at 11:30 to meet with them for 45 minutes because you have an idea or project you are working on with which you need some specific help.

Take the time between the request to meet and the actual meeting to plan out very specifically- as best you know how- how you will invite them to join the team. Let them know the idea behind the assignment. Give them the final deadline. Share who else is on the team. Let them know what kind of resources are available.

This speaks their language. It lets them know you understand the significance of logistics in the real world, and it will entice them to say "yes" to your invitation.

DELEGATOR

Every team needs a Delegator. By virtue of their leadership "D," you probably only need one. Two would probably trip all over themselves. Trust me when I say that, if you need another Delegator on the team, the first one knows one and stands a better chance than you do of getting them for you.

Delegators are the glue which holds the team together relationally. They will help you navigate relationships and all their complexities. They can motivate when others cannot. They can mend when others cannot.

Add a Delegator to your team, and you don't just get them... You get everyone they know whom you might need going forward.

FIND DELEGATORS:
Delegators are relational. In my opinion, they should be the easiest to spot. The old school ones have a massive rolodex on their desk. The new school ones have hundreds, if not thousands, of contacts on their smartphone.

Get on social media and locate someone you think might be a Delegator. Look at how they interact with people. Find those people who always have other people in the pictures with them and not just selfies.

Delegators are about doing life together with other people. And it's not just a work thing for them. Who never goes shopping alone? Who is always inviting some group of people to go out to eat after church? Who vacations with family and friends?

At work, find who always seems to have a meaningful conversation going on... at the water cooler or on the phone. Find that person who has more emails from more people in their inbox (not ads from stores) than should be humanly possible, and you are probably honing in on a Delegator.

I mentioned earlier that I like to fish. More than a decade ago, I had a friend who had a friend who owned some land with a couple ponds on it. My friend took me fishing several times there over the years, and we always caught fish. In fact, on my most prolific fishing trip ever, he and I combined to catch and keep 88 fish, not counting the ones we threw back. Now, I've gone fishing in plenty of places where I've not caught one fish. But at that pond, the least we ever caught was eight good bass. We always caught fish there.

Here's the thing, if you're going to catch fish, you have to fish where the fish are. Do that, and you'll always catch fish. In the same way, find where the people are, and you will definitely be able to catch a Delegator there because they are people-people and so they are always where the people are.

ATTRACT DELEGATORS:
In case you missed it before, Delegators are relational. If you want to add a Delegator to your team, you are going to have to sell them on the "who" of the assignment. Who does it benefit or help? Who is on the team already? Who else would you like to get to help you out, but can't seem to connect with?

Delegators are not interested in the plan or the details other than how they can connect and involve more people in the process. An old African proverb says, "If you want to go fast, go alone. If you want to go far, go together." The Delegator always wants to go far, no matter how slow the pace. It's about people for them.

Try to not overthink this. Show them the people they will get to connect with. Show them how their connections will help connect people with other people. Show them people, and you will attract them.

INVITE DELEGATORS:
Delegators are relational. Do yourself a favor and skip the text or email on this invitation. Be purposefully personal.

While you were super strategic with the Developer, you almost have to create the illusion that the invitation to the Delegator happened spontaneously. I'm not talking about being deceptive here. I'm simply saying that if you come across as all business and too impersonal, they will not be interested.

Start with small talk. I like to joke with people that since I am from the South, I like to deal with situations by sitting around on the front porch, sipping iced tea, beating around the bush and almost brushing up against the subject at hand. Then I walk away from the conversation thinking to myself, "Well, I'm glad we talked about that!"

While that concept drives some people nuts and sometimes doesn't seem to accomplish much, it might actually gain you brownie points with the Delegator and see you land them on your team. Don't be opposed to having two or three conversations before actually "popping the question."

If you'll give a Delegator a chance to know you a little, you just might find that they are more likely to join your happy little band of amazing individuals... and you'll find that your team just got better because you added a Delegator!

BONUS NOTE: If it were me, I would probably start with the Delegator as the first person I would attempt to add to my team so that they could help me in my search for the others.

DOER

Every team needs a Doer. Truth be told, this is the one area of your team where it is fine to have a lot of leaders. Depending on what your assignment or project or event requires, the number of Doers you need to get the job done varies. Regardless of what you are trying to accomplish, though, it is usually very difficult to have too many Doers.

Some people think of Doers as a-dime-a-dozen. Others value them highly as those who "get the job done." Some dismiss

Doers as followers only and not leaders. Others recognize that Doers are leaders who simply have a different leadership "D" designation... a different way of leading. Your perception of these leaders will determine how easily you find them, attract them and add them to your team.

Doers are in many ways the anchor leg of your team's race. Others may dream, tweak, plan and connect, but if your team lacks Doers, it is akin to running every lap except the final, finishing lap in a four by one hundred relay race.

Enlist Doers and you instantly escalate the chances of your team accomplishing its goals exponentially.

FIND DOERS:

Doers are functional. To find these leaders, you are going to have to look in some different places. Get to the time clock 15-20 minutes early because they are likely to be clocking in before others. Stay late after a church social and find those people washing dishes or putting tables away because Doers aren't quitting till the work is done and the task list is completely checked off.

To find Doers, you have to go where the work is. They may or may not initially feel as if they have time to stop and talk with you. In fact, don't be surprised if they tell you that they will be happy to talk with you if you will "grab the other end of that box" or "hop in the car and go with me to pick up this person at the airport."

I mentioned fishing earlier. Sometimes certain fish school or gather in a specific area. When you find them, you can usually "load the boat" with fish. The same can be true of finding Doers. This is a bonus for you because you may be able to add multiple players to your team with one stop.

Again, don't discount Doers as grunt labor. Though you may find them in the loading bay or the catwalk, there are some strong leaders there who can add significant value to your team if you are willing to go find them. When I say, "go find them," I mean it literally. You are not going to find them through email or social media. They don't have time to stop for a power lunch. Locating these team members is going to mean a little wear on the shoe leather.

ATTRACT DOERS:
Doers are functional. The key to being able to hand them a task list related to your assignment is to sell them on the "when and where" of the assignment. Let them know you have a list a mile long that you could never complete on your own.

Specifics are what they need to hear from you. They need to know that you need 2,000 chairs set up in 30 minutes for that next conference session.

I use that illustration because it's real to me. I was once leading a conference for a couple thousand students and the manager of the arena we were using tried to tell me that we couldn't use the floor space for inflatable games, etc. and still turn it back around to use for the next general session because his crew wasn't large enough on that holiday weekend and there simply wouldn't be time.

When I asked him if I would be allowed to handle it if his crew who was going to be there would help, he still balked. What he didn't understand... and what I finally had to prove to him... is that I had recruited an army of about 100 Doers who would absolutely be able to turn that arena around from one use to the other. He finally relented to allow us to give it a shot. And we finally proved what Doers can do when they are given a goal and a list.

It wasn't hard for me to garner those Doers for that event because it made sense that I needed their help to accomplish something otherwise impossible. They loved the challenge of doing at their peak potential to help a dream become reality. Doers are functional leaders who enjoy seeing the small results which add up to major results.

To attract Doers, you need a goal too large for one person or one small group of people to accomplish alone... a list a mile long... a location and time to show up... and a deadline to complete the tasks. Do that, and you will find that Doers are intrigued enough to check it out.

INVITE DOERS:

Did I happen to mention that Doers are functional? This may be the simplest of all the invitations for people to join your team. How great is that? The leaders you need in multitude are the ones who are easiest to ask.

The plan here is to keep it simple, straightforward and short. Seriously, don't overthink this. Don't overdo it. No glitz, no glamor. Just a simple, clearly defined invitation to join the team. Skip the dream and the impact.

Your time to make the request will most likely be limited. Make the most of it. Come prepared with a few specifics about what you would need done and how you cannot do it without their help. Let them know that you realize they are busy, and that's why you chose them. Let them know that you value the contribution you feel they could make to the team. Show them your to-do list, and as you wrap up the conversation... in less than three minutes hopefully... ask them for a response. If they cannot give you an answer right then, ask them to add it to their to-do list for tomorrow or later in the week. Trust me, they have a to-do list, and they will love adding one more thing to it to check off.

In the movie *That Thing You Do,* actor Tom Hanks portrays a manager for an up and coming band in the 1960's. At a state fair, he instructs the band to go on stage, play their hit song, unplug and get off the stage. One of the band members asks what to do if the crowd loves it and wants more. Tom Hanks' character reiterates his directive to go out, play the song, unplug and get off the stage.

My suggestion to you in inviting a Doer to join your team is this... Go out, make your pitch, ask them to join your team, thank them and walk away. You may be wondering what to do if... Let me say it again... Go out, make your pitch, ask them to join your team and walk way.

If you'll do this, you will find that Doers are attracted to what it is you're proposing and will be excited to be a part of it. And when you add Doers to the team, you know that your team just got way better.

I loved watching the *Mission Impossible* television series which aired in the mid 1960's to the early 1970's. I obviously watched re-runs, thank you very much. The running plot was basically that a leader would be assigned what seemed like a very challenging, if not impossible, task to accomplish. I think what I loved most about the show was how that leader found the right people to do the right parts of the assignment to achieve success. One person was a master at disguise and impersonating other people. Another person was a demolitions expert. Still another was a tech-wizard.

It is this concept around which the idea of finding, attracting and inviting other people to join our teams finds similarity. Regardless of what your assignment is, you need a team in order for it to be the most successful it possibly can. You have to be able to identify the right potential team members, convince them that they want to be a part of what your team is going to attempt, and secure their participation. And you can do it!

People are there for the finding. People want to be found. People make themselves findable. If you will open your eyes and mind to the tell-tale signs they are hanging out for you, you will find the very people you need on your team.

People want to feel wanted, needed and valued. I realize I'm making some pretty big assumptions that you understand you have to show people appreciation beyond pay... that you know you have to give people recognition for a job well-done... that you are clear on the fact that you have to, in some meaningful way, compensate people (not just pay them money) for their helping you accomplish your goal. Do that and you will attract them.

People want to be asked in a clear, understandable manner which truly conveys your heart behind the invitation and the significance of what you hope to accomplish. Do that, and you will discover that the right people will almost always say "yes" to your invitation.

CONCLUSION

YOU DID IT! You finished this book. Let me be the first to congratulate you. There are plenty of people who never finish reading one book a year, let alone as quickly as you finished this one. And before you set this down, I would love to share some parting thoughts.

I was listening recently to the "SiriusXM Blitz" on the NFL Network channel on satellite radio in our vehicle. As I write this, we are in the off season for the NFL. So, there is no discussion about how a particular game went this week, or which team might make it to the playoffs.

Instead, all the talk is about teams trading players, players retiring, and the upcoming NFL Draft for teams to get new players. As I listened to the show, the hosts were discussing which players various teams had lost and how they needed to add players to make up for those losses in the off season.

One of the hosts mentioned the phrase, "missing pieces," and it caught my attention because that is the thrust of this book. Too many leaders are trying to play every position themselves, or at best, leading a team which is "missing pieces." But it takes a complete team to compete effectively and win. It takes a really great, well thought-out, strategically crafted team to accomplish something significant.

Great teams have no "missing pieces." I'm not talking about talent or recognition. There are NFL teams who embrace a "next man up" philosophy which basically means that when the best player out there gets hurt and has to be replaced, the next player in that position must step up their game and play at the level necessary to help the team win. The key here is that these teams always have depth... they are not ever "missing pieces." So they consistently win as a team.

As we come to the end of this book, I have a couple of take-aways I hope for you to grab hold of. I don't necessarily expect you to always remember the names of the five leadership "D" designations off the top of your head. You can always go back and reference this book for that.

And while I'd love for you to recall the techniques I recommend here, there are two much deeper realizations which I hope you have come to grab hold of in a subtle, underlying way as you've read. They are the heart behind the head-knowledge provided in this book and the impetus for writing it.

Though they are so simple that you might be tempted to roll your eyes at me upon reading them, my hope is that you will take them to heart... embrace them... make them part of your own leadership philosophy... and put them to work for your own benefit and the benefit of those you serve, as well as those you lead...

1. Believe that you can lead, and others need you.
Value yourself as a leader. You are full of potential. You have something your organization, your company, your church, your team... even your family... needs.

Believe that you have been given a gift to lead that your team needs. You have been given a leadership "D" that is not a score of how well you produce based on someone else's metrics, but rather a designation that denotes you have something to bring to the table which will help bring about success.

Too many of us lack the sense that we can contribute to something. We fail to recognize that, when we are on the team, the team is better than if we were not on it.

Others are counting on you. They need your talent, your gifts, your knowledge, your relationships, your skill set, your expertise. They need you.

It's not wrong to believe that you have value. It's only wrong when you think you're the only one who has value. Which leads us to the second takeaway from the heart of this book...

2. Believe that others can lead, too, and you need them.

Value others as leaders. I mean everyone. I truly believe anyone can lead when they know and operate in their God-given leadership "D." Believe that others have value and giftedness to bring to the team which can help your team succeed.

Too often, we undervalue people because they are not like us. Too often, we undervalue people because they lack a certain level of education or experience. Too often, we undervalue people because we don't believe they have performed to the level we expected of them.

But we also have to consider whether or not they know what their leadership "D" is and if they are being given the opportunity to function in that designation. Perhaps no one gives them the opportunity to shine in the way they were intended to shine.

As a leader, you have the ability to call out greatness in people by helping them discover that they have been given a leadership "D". You also have the privilege of setting them up to win by adding them to your team and allowing them to function in their leadership "D."

You can never go wrong by believing in people and helping them to succeed... because when they succeed, so do you.

I believe that if you will embrace the truth that you have received a "D" in leadership... and so has everyone else... then you will believe that anyone can lead with excellence. So, get out there... find those "missing pieces" of your team... and build a team who will lead like never before!

NOTES

Introduction
1. "44 Inspiring John C. Maxwell Quotes for Leadership Success, accessed at Inc.com on 11-29-16

Chapter 1 - Everyone Gets a "D"
2. Graphic quote found on blog at healthyfitfocused.com, Monday, September 15, 2014, accessed 04-27-17

Chapter 2 - Dreamers

Chapter 3 - Designers

Chapter 4 - Developers

Chapter 5 - Delegators

Chapter 6 - Doers
3. Pin saved from www.squidoo.com, viewed on Pinterest on 4-27-17

Chapter 7 - Take The Quiz

Chapter 8 - Find, Attract & Invite The Right "D's"
4. goodreads.com, Phil Jackson quote on strength of the team, accessed on 08-21-17

Conclusion

ACKNOWLEDGMENTS

I'D LIKE TO thank the following team members for their part in moving this book from a dream into reality:

- *Angela, Alex and Austin… for giving me the time to pursue this dream*
- *Jessica Horton and Lea Ann Pelt… for lending their editing skills to make the dream better*
- *Rod Whitlock… for guidance in the publishing process of how to make the dream become reality*
- *Chris Deville… for bringing the amazing cover design to cradle this dream*
- *Brandon Anders… for helping me work through the development of the quiz so that others can embrace the dream for themselves*
- *All my family and friends… for encouraging me along the way to keep dreaming and keep writing*

- *And most importantly, the Lord… for giving me the dream, desire, ability and opportunity to write*

About The Author

ALLEN CHAPIN IS the passionately committed husband to Angela, whom he met at Southwestern Assemblies of God University, and to whom he has been happily married for more than 22 years. He is also the wildly proud dad of two sons, Alex and Austin.

Allen enjoys eating natural peanut butter by the spoonful, fishing for crappie and bream on light tackle, reminiscing about 1980's nostalgia and watching NFL football.

He is also an ordained minister with the Assemblies of God, having served that fellowship in a variety of leadership roles through local churches, at one of the fellowship's premier universities, and as a statewide director.

Allen also authors a blog called "Up: Encouragement and Motivation for Living Up In An Often Down World" which can be found at allenchapin.com.

Connect
With Allen

To CONNECT WITH Allen with comments, questions or invitations to speak, feel free to utilize the following:

Email:
achapin70@gmail.com

Facebook:
facebook.com/allenangelachapin

Twitter & Instagram:
achapin70

Personal Thoughts
& Great Quotes